# KUNDALINI
# AWAKENING

# KUNDALINI AWAKENING

A Gentle Guide to
Chakra Activation
and Spiritual Growth

JOHN SELBY

*Conceived and painted by*
ZACHARY ZELIG

BANTAM BOOKS NEW YORK TORONTO LONDON SYDNEY AUCKLAND

KUNDALINI AWAKENING

*A Bantam Book/September 1992*

*Library of Congress Cataloging-in-Publication Data*

Selby, John.
   Kundalini awakening : a gentle guide to chakra activation and
spiritual growth / by John Selby ; illustrated by Zachary Zelig.
      p.   cm.
   Includes bibliographical references and index.
   ISBN 0-553-35330-6
   1. New Age movement.   2. Kundalinī.   3. Chakras.   I. Title.
BP605.N48S45   1992
294.5'43—dc20                                                    92-4737
                                                                      CIP

*Published simultaneously in the United States and Canada*

*Bantam Books are published by Bantam Books, a division of Bantam Doubleday Dell*
*Publishing Group, Inc. Its trademark, consisting of the words "Bantam Books" and the*
*portrayal of a rooster, is Registered in U.S. Patent and Trademark Office and in other*
*countries. Marca Registrada. Bantam Books, 1540 Broadway, New York, New York 10036.*

# ACKNOWLEDGMENTS

The chakra series of paintings was created over a four-year span of time in Tucson, Arizona. I am indebted to my fellow artist, Jon Lightfoot, and the Light of Southern Arizona that activated the creation of the series of paintings in *Kundalini Awakening*.

To my dear friend Baroness Kristine von Jutrcenka I owe thanks for the support and encouragement she gave me with watchful care during my apprenticeship with my Masters in the remote regions of Mexico and Peru, and the time spent at the Krotona Institute in Ojai, California, with her.

I am honored to have had the guidance and direction of one of Latin America's great British Surrealist painters, the late Bridget Bates Tichnor. I owe great thanks to the years of dedicated friendship and the infinite wisdom that she mirrored back to me as my mentor, from my early years in Mexico and in New York at Parsons and the New York Art Students League until her death in 1990.

There have been many people in "the Healing Arts" that have assisted me in clearing my path in life—physically, emotionally, mentally, and spiritually. To Charles Nunn from the Edgar Cayce Foundation, I give thanks for my own personal expansion through the Chakras Past-Life Regression work we did in Apache Canyon, New Mexico.

As one moves forward in the realm of full spectrum alignment with kundalini in the physical body, it becomes necessary that all separations of "self" are cleared and transmuted. It is only then that one's personal integrity harmonizes with the kundalini process. I want to thank Caroline Conley in Los Angeles for the three years I worked with her in clearing and transmuting my own separations. Without her training I would not be in "wholeness" to bring forth the true essence of the material in this book as it applies to grounded Earth Consciousness and transmutation.

To my extraordinary parents, Eleanor and Marvin Selig, I owe to them the opportunity to have formulated my life through their committed nourishment. Love is the seed for all growth and compassion is our greatest ally.

I would like to thank my friends Brenda Venus and Henry Bushkin for guiding *Kundalini Awakening* to Peter Miller, my literary agent. I extend my gratitude to Peter for his patience in the publication of this book. In addition, I am most grateful for the collaborative work of my editors at Bantam, Leslie Meredith and Claudine Murphy.

And to all of my Masters and Guides . . . Thank you!

*Zachary Zelig*
*Paris, France*
*May 28, 1991*


In memory, with enduring love, to Thakin Kung, Krishnamurti, Alan Watts, and Rebecca Oriard.

*John Selby*
*Kilauea, Hawaii*
*March 1992*

# Contents

# Introduction

*Within the great spiritual* traditions of the world there exists the wise teaching that at any given moment we are always being confronted with exactly what we need to experience, in order to progress into a higher level of mystic realization. This means that if only we tune in, the universe at this very moment is offering us access to the specific spiritual insights and instructions we're presently ready to encounter.

I remember vividly how this seemingly magical process brought kundalini meditation to my attention back in 1966, one cold November night at Princeton University where I was studying at the time. Perhaps if I share with you the drama of my own initial exposure to kundalini consciousness, you may sense directly the spiritual excitement and promise of the meditation techniques we will be exploring in this book.

I'd made plans that night to have an early dinner with a good friend. At the appointed hour I went running up two flights of dormitory steps and into his room, without bothering to knock. Quite unexpectedly, I found myself in the presence of a lovely woman, sitting cross-legged on my roommate's bed, her spine straight and her eyes closed, with the most remarkable, radiant expression on her face.

I stood awestruck in front of her. I'd seen pictures of various paintings and statues of ancient Buddhas in the act of deep contemplation. But having grown up in a cattle-ranching environment where Oriental meditation simply didn't exist, I'd never before encountered a real live person fully immersed in such a potent state of inner reflection.

This woman in front of me, sitting with her hands palms-up on her knees, her breasts rising and falling slowly and evenly with deep full breaths, her lips relaxed in a Mona Lisa smile—I immediately recognized that there was something extraordinary going on inside her. She seemed to be almost visibly broadcasting some sort of inner spiritual peace and energy. I felt face-to-face with something radically new—something that evoked both fright and intense fascination inside me.

As I stood there staring at her, before I could regain my composure and turn to leave so as not to disturb her meditation, her eyes slowly opened and looked directly into mine. Neither of us spoke a word. I felt momentarily transported beyond normal levels of consciousness. Her expression expanded into a friendly, beatific smile. I experienced a most peculiar and extremely pleasurable sensation in my heart region—a feeling that I would come to know more intimately when I began my own kundalini training.

The sound of footsteps coming up the stairs outside the room brought us back to more customary states of mind. My friend came running in, introducing the young woman as his sister from the West Coast, who had arrived unexpectedly. With little more said, we went off to dinner.

Somewhere between salad and baked potatoes, the woman started telling her brother about a spiritual teacher from Asia with whom she was studying—a quite young but already fully enlightened man who'd radically altered her understanding of life. Her brother, a physics major who considered such esoteric topics the height of nonscientific foolishness, immediately made a joke of her confession. She accepted his harsh attack without arguing, and said no more about her new spiritual path.

I for my part, having observed firsthand the blissful, transcendent state her meditative technique had moved her into an hour before, was all ears to find out what sort of mental tricks could induce such an illumined condition. When her brother excused himself to attend an evening lecture, I encouraged her to talk further about her spiritual explorations.

"Well, the technique that I'm practicing is called kundalini meditation," she said.

"I've never heard the word before," I confessed. "What's it mean?"

"*Kundalini's* a very old term," she explained, "from the Sanskrit language of ancient India. It refers to the basic lifeforce that's inside all of us."

"So you meditate on your lifeforce?"

"That's where we begin. Kundalini energy's infinite, but it's mostly blocked in our bodies. We don't need very much to survive physically."

"So what's the purpose of your meditating?"

"Well," she said, reflecting a moment. "It's to open up and experience who I am more deeply—to encourage more lifeforce energy to flow through my body. It's based on the fact that we all have seven subtle energy centers in our bodies. Kundalini meditation is a powerful, and pleasurable, way to wake them all up."

"So how exactly do you do that—wake them up?"

"I'm only just beginning to learn," she said, again smiling her special smile. "You'd have to meet my Master to find out. It's a deep process."

Seven months later, having read several rather difficult esoteric books about kundalini meditation that the young lady had kindly sent to me in the interim, I flew to San Francisco to visit her. We went the following morning to a house where I could meet her Master, a young man from Burma named Thakin Kung.

I was immediately struck by the particular quality of personal presence this man emanated. He was only five or six years older than I was, but he possessed a sense of inner certainty, of personal power, of heartfelt compassion that bowled me over. I sat down in the back of the room. About thirty people were meditating cross-legged on pillows. During the next hour, just by being in the presence of such an advanced kundalini teacher, I experienced a spontaneous rush of intense spiritual energy throughout my body that amazed me.

The next few weeks were like an idyllic dream in comparison with my usual life at Princeton. That summer of 1967 in San Francisco was the early blossoming of the spiritual and sexual revolution that was soon to sweep the country. My own experience proved to be a microcosm of the whole, as I went twice a day to study kundalini with the young Master, and also entered into a most beautiful sexual relationship with the woman who had first introduced me to kundalini.

Then, my vacation time over, back I went to my normal life with all its constant obligations and usual drudgeries. I'd had a taste in San Francisco of something marvelous, something utterly remark-able—the personal realization that we're more than just physical bodies, that we can actually tune directly into the infinite wisdom and power of the universe if we master certain meditation techniques that encourage communion with the divine.

I found, however, that without the constant support of my San Francisco kundalini group, it was extremely difficult to maintain the heightened spiritual states of clarity and inner power that I'd encoun-tered briefly and now hungered for. I searched urgently for another meditation Master to study with, but found no one with whom I felt compatible.

## OUR INNER MASTER

One of the stark realities of modern life is that there are very few true spiritual Masters in Western society to whom we can turn for inspiration and instruction in kundalini meditation. And all too often, the Masters we do find are teaching an extreme path that is beyond our everyday ability to participate in.

I remember reaching a state of deep confusion and depression back at Princeton, yearning for my Master's presence, feeling sorry for myself for being separated from my source of spiritual inspiration and instruction. I had read in one of my many esoteric books that without a Master, no one can progress on the spiritual path. Since I could find no kundalini teacher at Princeton, I felt completely shut off from the world of spirit.

Then one fateful night a well-known spiritual writer named Alan Watts lectured on campus, and I talked with him afterwards about my plight. Alan, who eventually became a close friend of mine, took me aside for a few moments. The words that he said have ever since reverberated within me:

"John," he said, "don't fool yourself. You are your own Master. We're all Masters. We all possess a higher self deep within us that's infinite, that's one with the All. Meditation is the process where we realize this. All you have to do is learn to look inside instead of outside all the time—open yourself to your own inner Master. That's the real trick of meditation."

In perfect accordance with the spiritual notion I mentioned earlier—that we are always being given the lesson we're ready to learn—Alan had appeared just when I needed him, right when I was ready to learn that crucial lesson. And as I'm writing this book, I'm assuming the same for you—that you haven't come upon this particular book of kundalini meditation purely by chance, but rather hold it in your hands right now because you're ready to learn a potent way to advance into deeper communion with your own infinite spiritual presence.

Even though we all have our inner Master to aid us in our spiritual explorations, it's always, in practical experience, the combination of external suggestions and guidance, along with internal guidance from our spiritual center, that generates the momentum of spiritual growth. We do need help from the outside, both general inspiration and also concrete suggestions regarding effective meditation techniques. Books often provide this help and guidance.

## WRITTEN WORDS THAT ENCOURAGE SPIRITUAL GROWTH

It's been my observation that all really good writing is by definition inspired writing. When a writer/teacher allows his or her inner Master to influence what is being written, words gain a special power and spirit that can genuinely evoke transformation.

When you read an author's words and feel somehow moved by the experience, this is because the higher Self of the writer is communicating directly with your own higher Self. Such is the underlying magic of both the written and the spoken word.

My intent in writing this book has been to channel into concrete verbal form the meditative wisdom and pragmatic techniques I've encountered during my own spiritual explorations, so that you can make intimate contact with the heart of kundalini meditation in your own life. I've designed the book to communicate on several different levels at once, depending on your own spiritual state of expansion. If you've never before explored a meditative practice, you will find the basic background information and instructions needed to begin the inner journey to your spiritual center. If you already have previous meditation experience, this book will provide advanced levels of instruction and insight to encourage your spiritual evolution.

The structure of this book is the result of the last fifteen years or so, during which I've been teaching students and clients how to approach kundalini awakening in a safe, gentle, enjoyable way. I'm very thankful to the many people who've helped me refine this program into its present shape and clarity, and I am pleased that you can now benefit from their input.

## KUNDALINI MEDITATION

As you know, many different meditative traditions have come into being throughout the world during the last five thousand years, developing specific theologies and rituals through countless generations of deep spiritual exploration. In spite of their seeming differences, all these meditative traditions have one goal in common—that of bringing human beings into more direct experiential contact with the spiritual realities of the universe.

By definition, there can be only one Infinite Presence, one Universal Creative Source, one all-encompassing Consciousness for us to tap into. So even though the various human civilizations have developed quite diverse ways for approaching spiritual reality, the Infinite Presence we seek communion with is always the same.

The reason kundalini meditation is such a remarkable process for spiritual awakening is that it is not based on complex theological arguments, or culturally defined religious concepts. Kundalini meditation is focused instead upon the immediate, ultimate experience of the divine within all of us, not upon belief systems regarding that divinity. Therefore, regardless of our particular religious upbringing and theological beliefs, all of us can employ kundalini meditation to aid in our spiritual evolution. Once we learn to look beyond concepts, we are free to encounter—through direct spiritual illumination—the radiant core of Love and Life that lies at the center of our own personal consciousness.

# KUNDALINI IN WORLD HISTORY

The Hindu meditative tradition of ancient India was the original source of present-day kundalini meditation techniques. At least four thousand years ago, a number of great spiritual Masters developed what later came to be known as the Yogic path to mystic illumination. This path included the regular practice of physical movements and hatha-yoga postures, concerted breathing meditations, acts of devotion in one's community, the chanting of certain sounds and evocative words, meditating upon visual images, and focusing upon the seven energy centers, or "chakras," that lie up and down the human spine.

Kundalini meditation was considered the highest form of this ancient Yogic tradition of spiritual development. In many different variations and levels of intensity, it is still practiced throughout the Orient in both the Hindu and the Buddhist traditions by many millions of people. However, only in the last few generations has this vast spiritual tradition become available to Western people seeking the pragmatic "nuts and bolts," the pure experiential process, of spiritual awakening.

The reason kundalini meditation possesses such universal appeal at this point in history is that it offers a clear, experience-based approach for awakening our mundane minds to the presence of our true spiritual nature. Through kundalini meditation we can master the quieting of our habitual flows of thoughts, which normally block deep spiritual reflection. Then in this calm state of consciousness, we can observe and participate in the infinite lifeforce as it flows through our bodies. And with regular meditation, we come to experience a most remarkable phenomenon directly at the center of our own being—the bright flash of illumination that brings us into immediate contact with the divine force of creation that animates all of life.

# Freeing Kundalini from Esoteric Overtones

I was lucky enough to have a grandfather who was himself a deep spiritual Master, even though, as an old-time cattle rancher, he certainly never took on that role in any formal fashion. What he taught, or more precisely what he showed through his own life's example, was that to live life fully, we must learn to let go of all our chronic thought flows, all our convoluted religious concepts, all our superstitious fantasies and theological belief systems—and encounter the depths and heights of spiritual life directly, through our immediate experience.

Even while I was getting my doctorate in comparative religions and training in formal therapy traditions, I was still regularly returning to Grandad's ranch to sit quietly with the old man, listen intently when he spoke, and nurture the qualities of contemplation he radiated. In reflection, I can see that his spiritual example was what enabled me to sense immediately, when I first encountered kundalini meditation, that here was a process that offered essential keys for advancing rapidly in spiritual directions.

His example also made me react and pull back from much of the esoteric baggage kundalini authors and teachers often present. If you've heard of kundalini meditation before reading this book, you've almost certainly heard of it as being a highly esoteric tradition, extremely difficult to master, even downright dangerous to explore. The public press has promoted this distorted image of kundalini meditation because it makes for a good story. I remember reading, for instance, that kundalini energy is like atomic energy—that it has vast powers, and if not handled with extreme caution, it can cause serious damage to the nervous system when unleashed. And, of course, in extreme situations with already unbalanced individuals, this is close to the truth. There are always extremes to be avoided in exploring potent systems of meditation.

Luckily, my first introduction to kundalini awakening was

through one of the few true Masters who has come to the West with a reasonable, nonesoteric, completely safe approach to kundalini meditation. This man, Thakin Kung, whom I mentioned earlier, was in our midst only for a few intense years as a public teacher of kundalini awakening. But his remarkably practical approach to the ancient kundalini teachings, mellowed by his Burmese interpretation of the Indian and Tibetan tradition, has been spread throughout our contemporary spiritual community by the lives and teachings of his students.

In this book I want to make this practical, nonesoteric approach to kundalini illumination available in a form that we can all readily tune in to and apply to our everyday lives. I've regularly taught these meditative techniques both to spiritual students and also to therapy clients, and in the process of teaching have developed a step-by-step presentation that makes Thakin's meditative process relevant and applicable to our current everyday life.

Especially, I've removed the remaining religious overtones found in Thakin's teachings, so you don't have to adopt any new religious orientation in order to embrace these meditative programs in your own life. Kundalini is a power, a presence, an illumination that lies beyond human religious thought. We need no religious symbology dragging us down in our exploration of our deeper spiritual nature. All we need are core meditative techniques that enable us to quiet our thinking minds so we become still, and know through immediate personal contact our oneness with God—with whatever name we might give to the infinite and yet intimate spiritual presence that lives deep within us.

## THE ANCIENT MEANING OF KUNDALINI

Many thousand years ago in Hindu mythology there was a sexually charged goddess called Kundalini. This goddess was said to exist in the form of a sleeping serpent, wrapped around the base of the spine, awaiting the opportunity to awaken and rise up through all the seven energy centers, or *chakras*, charging each of them with transformative insight and power.

In harmony with this ancient myth, the Sanskrit word *kundalini* can be traced back to its root term *kundala*, which means "coiled." Evolving through the generations, kundalini came to refer to the latent power of spiritual realization buried deep down in the human body, perpetually under pressure to rise up and manifest its ultimate truths, power, and bliss.

In one of the first kundalini books I read (Sir John Woodroffe's *The Serpent Power*, which stands as a classic on the topic), kundalini awakening was said to happen when our individual kundalini consciousness rises up the spine and merges with the infinite, cosmic, eternal kundalini. In Western terminology, this same experience is referred to as mystic communion with the divine—as we come fully alive to our full spiritual potential.

## INTEGRATING KUNDALINI AWAKENING INTO CONTEMPORARY LIFE

Traditionally in India, Tibet, and outlying regions where kundalini meditation was taught, a devout student was required to put aside all worldly desires and aspirations, and under the constant guidance of an enlightened Master, concentrate totally upon attaining the ultimate state of absolute, permanent union with the divine.

Under the guidance of an advanced Yogic teacher, I followed this extreme path myself at an early point in my development— shortly after Thakin Kung departed for his homeland. I did my best to divorce myself from Western tradition, and to take on the Hindu mind-state and approach to spiritual discipline.

During these amazing two years of my life, I did have a number of very powerful kundalini breakthroughs. But ultimately, for me, adapting the Hindu mentality required a shift of consciousness that was too extreme. I came to accept that I was deeply rooted in my own culture—and for a spiritual path to work for me, it had to be integrated into my own cultural heritage. Exploring esoteric traditions of other civilizations proved worthwhile to a point, but when it came to the actual process of attaining illumination in everyday life, I hungered for a path that wouldn't force me to deny any of my own heritage, in order to awaken my kundalini energy.

Step by step, I discovered during ensuing years of study and meditation that the primary techniques of kundalini awakening can be successfully separated from their cultural background. Rather than trying to stuff our spiritual experience into foreign mind-states and religious symbology, we can put aside esoteric mind-games, look to our own inner Master for guidance, practice particular meditative techniques that apply to all human beings and all historic ages, and reap the spiritual benefits that come to us. This seems to be the wise path, the moderate path, the contemporary kundalini path to spiritual illumination.

## SCIENCE AND THE CHAKRAS

In the kundalini tradition, there are seven distinct energy centers known to exist in the human body, located up and down the spine and also in the brain itself. In Sanskrit terminology, the energy centers have traditionally been called *chakras*. These internal energy vortexes are not only grand symbolic notions. They are in fact definite energetic happenings inside each of our bodies—whether we're aware of them or not.

In the ancient Hindu spiritual understanding, these chakras were said to be empowered by a mysterious force called *prana*, which the human body takes in regularly through breathing. In a more contemporary scientific understanding, the inner energy vortexes empowering the human organism are understood in terms of the electromagnetic dynamics of subatomic physics. The chakras are in fact a primal expression of the cosmic dance described by subatomic physicists as a spontaneous shifting of matter into energy, energy into matter, and matter back to energy again.

As Einstein clearly posited—and ancient Yogic Masters knew many thousands of years before—our bodies are not just material in nature. They are also quite definitely energetic in nature. Science has amassed considerable knowledge concerning this electromagnetic, Bioenergetic functioning of the human body. But scientists are first to admit that they don't really comprehend the underlying forces that generate life. Scientific instruments can look only so far into the matter-energy continuum, before reaching their perceptual limits.

However, as "spiritual experimenters" have known for thousands of years, the human mind itself is in fact capable of focusing directly upon the creative source of life. Consciousness has proven itself to be the ultimate tool for encountering and participating in the underlying forces that empower our lives, as we commune directly with the basic scientific realities of life.

Kundalini meditation is a specific, quite precise technique for awakening the conscious mind to the presence of the seven energetic centers—or chakras—in the body. Through focusing regularly on these energy centers, we learn to balance our energetic system for optimum functioning, while also increasing the overall flow of energy through all seven chakras, so that our entire being becomes illumined.

## KUNDALINI AND SEXUAL AWAKENING

The popular press has often fixated upon the particular aspect of kundalini meditation that is overtly sexual. It is quite true that kundalini energy is grounded in our personal creative energy, which is sexual in nature. My own initiation into kundalini meditation, as I mentioned before, was combined with a very powerful and beautiful sexual relationship in which my female friend and I employed our wild rushing sexual charges for expanded spiritual progress.

Kundalini meditation increases our capacity to experience intense bliss and pleasure in all that we do. Because sexual intercourse is the ultimate union of male and female energies in the creative act, this is certainly a prime place where kundalini energy is experienced.

All the kundalini Masters I have known, however, have emphasized that a person must first tune into his or her own inner spiritual energies and conscientiously devote time to solitary meditation. Only then comes a heightened sense of energization, pleasure, and heart-to-heart union during sexual intercourse.

Several traditional schools of kundalini meditation encourage the use of erotic fantasies in order to awaken the Kundalini Goddess from her sleeping state at the base of the spine. This "sexual fantasy" path might make sense for celibate monks studying under a great Master high in the Himalayas a thousand years ago. But my experience has been that in our modern world, employing erotic fantasies to stimulate the rising of kundalini energies up the spine is usually counterproductive. The purpose of kundalini meditation is not to generate a masturbatory rush of sexual energy through the system, but instead to consciously nurture a steady increase in our overall energetic condition.

Certainly as you progress with your kundalini meditations, you will experience an increase in sexual potency and pleasure. I encourage you to explore with your sexual partner, if you have one, the deepening intensities of orgasm that are brought about through the conscious awakening of your kundalini presence during meditation. But make your solitary meditation sessions primary, and receive the sexual manifestations as a gift of grace bestowed upon you.

## AVOIDING EXTREMES

I want to specifically address certain pitfalls sometimes encountered by kundalini meditators. Ever since the publication of Gopi Krishna's *Kundalini: The Evolutionary Energy in Man* several generations ago, in which this famous kundalini Master from India described his radical personal initiation into the fires of total kundalini awakening, too many writers and spiritual teachers have fixated on horror-story accounts of a few hapless individuals who have tapped spontaneously into a total kundalini awakening and suffered prolonged bouts of physical and emotional turmoil.

It is true, as I have known from working with a number of clients in my psychological practice, that sudden spontaneous kundalini awakening, especially in already unstable personalities, can be chaotic, frightening—even shattering to a person's normal life. Imagine what it's like to suddenly experience a hundred times more energy flowing through your body without any preparation or warning. This extreme is certainly not a desired aim of kundalini awakening.

I myself had several such experiences of radical unpremeditated kundalini uprising through my nervous system, before I was prepared meditatively to understand or properly channel such an upflow. In translating the ancient kundalini meditative techniques into contemporary form, my aim has been to guarantee that my students don't ever overamp their systems in such a manner.

In contrast, in the pages to come, you will find a program that leads you through a gentle, safe process of kundalini awakening, clearly avoiding the pitfalls that come to people who push too fast too soon into expanded levels of energization.

Many traditional approaches to kundalini awakening specifically aimed toward blasting a full surge of kundalini energy right up through all seven chakras, so that the top chakra, called the Crown Chakra, would be fully activated. For people seeking complete liberation from normal consciousness, once and forever, such an aim might make sense.

In this book, however, our aim is different. Rather than fixating overmuch on the seventh, ultimate chakra at the top of the head, we maintain the fourth, "middle" chakra, the heart/love center of our spiritual body, as our primary focus, and integrate the other six energy centers around this compassionate centerpoint. Rather than aiming to blast ourselves forever free from everyday human life, we're going to explore how to charge ourselves with radiant compassion and spiritual power that integrate perfectly into the routines of our contemporary lives.

## THE FOUR KEY MEDITATIVE TOOLS

Meditation in general, and certainly kundalini meditation in particular, should not be seen as a vague, mysterious process that lies beyond our normal awareness. What we do in the meditative experience is straightforward—we learn to focus our all-important power of attention in particular potent directions, so as to awaken areas of consciousness that lie dormant until consciously tuned into.

There are four primary ways to direct our power of attention toward illuminatory experience.

(1) First of all, we can turn our attention inward to our own moment-to-moment sensory experience of being alive in the present moment. We do this by focusing on our breathing, our heartbeat and pulse, the pull of gravity on our bodies, and our spontaneous whole-body awareness in the present moment.

(2) The second technique, or "vehicle," for carrying us deeper into contact with our spiritual selves is to focus our power of attention directly on each of the seven chakras in our bodies, so as to stimulate these energy centers into higher, more balanced levels of participation in the infinite dance of life.

(3) The third primary tool we will use in this program is the power of sound vibration—specifically, the power of our own voices to awaken each of the chakras up and down our spines. There are particular sounds, or

chants, called *mantras* in traditional Sanskrit terminology, that are associated with the awakening of each
of the energy centers. When we chant these sounds
either silently or aloud, we stimulate our deeper spiritual nature into higher levels of consciousness.

(4) The fourth vehicle for kundalini awakening is the use
of visual images for activating and balancing each of
the chakras. The noted transformational artist,
Zachary Zelig, with whom I collaborated in the
creation of the text, has created seven key chakra
paintings, known as *yantras* in traditional Hindu
practice, which provide the very essential impetus for
chakra activation.

During his fifteen years of study, meditation, and research into
the inner workings of yantra artwork, Zachary found that every great
civilization has developed specific geometric symbols and color com-
binations that are associated with the qualities of each of the energy
centers in the body. The paintings he has prepared for this book are
contemporary interpretations of these ancient yantra traditions. "To
relate totally with the diagram," Zachary explains, "is to unleash the
combined forces that each form represents." The paintings provide a
visual metaphysical alphabet or "thought forms" to help the reader
and viewer to focus internally and retain a color memory of the energy
encountered in meditation.

In Part II of the book, we will take each of the seven chakras in
turn and learn the particular visual image, vocal chant, focusing
technique, and breathing pattern that most powerfully and yet safely
awakens it. Then, once we have learned to effortlessly move through
the particular meditations on each chakra, we'll learn how to expand
our meditations to include all the chakras at once.

## IMMEDIATE AND LONG-TERM BENEFITS OF KUNDALINI MEDITATION

The meditations in this book, instead of being based on the "big bang" theory of spiritual awakening, are designed to bring about step-by-step illuminations that can be readily integrated into your everyday sense of identity. Each meditation you learn will encourage a movement in the direction of reduced anxiety and tension in your mind and body, and a concurrent increase in spiritual insight, sexual pleasure, mystic bliss, heightened self-awareness, and mystic communion.

Even in the preliminary meditations you will feel something changing, something expanding, something awakening in your deeper realms of being. As you learn to direct your awareness in new ways, you will immediately experience yourself as more "here." Your senses will awaken so that the present moment becomes truly multidimensional, full of new dimensions.

Many people begin meditation in a goal oriented mind-state, aiming toward some imaginary final state of total mystic realization and bliss. As you will discover quite quickly in this program, all such future-tripping is counterproductive. There is in fact no "future" to aim for in meditation. There is only the eternal present moment. It's rediscovery is the central theme of all meditation.

The great cosmic joke of all time is, of course, that we are already enlightened. In Christian terminology, we are already living in Christ Spirit. We are the Buddha, as they say in India. As the Zen tradition states so clearly, there is "nowhere to go, and nothing to do" to attain enlightenment—it is, we are, now.

Meditation can be seen as the process through which we rediscover our true identity beyond the confines of three-dimensional, chronological time. Each new step into this realization offers a flash of bliss, beauty, pleasure, and realization. Every new breath we breathe can thus be a breath of new life, of sudden self-discovery.

During his short period of public teaching in America, Thakin

Kung said so often that "if you are not fully enjoying your meditation in the present moment, you're not doing it in the proper spirit."

The "right" way to meditate is simply with a calm eagerness to look and see what is happening in your expanding consciousness right now. You are breathing in the present moment, so look to experience that reality. Your heart is beating, so look to experience that. Gravity is constantly causing you to dance the magnificent muscular dance of maintaining moment-to-moment balance—experience that. You have energy flows happening in your body—tune in to those flows. And you have an inner Master at the center of your being—tune in to its illuminatory presence.

Kundalini meditation is a magnificent, trustworthy, perfected technique for expanding into all these interrelated dimensions of human consciousness. It allows you to function, even in the midst of everyday life, as the perfect, illumined, sentient, conscious being you in essence are, even right now at this very moment.

It gives me great pleasure to offer this pragmatic approach to kundalini awakening, which you can explore, integrate into your present life, and use to awaken your own kundalini spirit. Especially during these traumatic times, we all carry the pressing responsibility to break free of our conditioned blinders and limitations, so that we can radiate the power of infinite love and wisdom in all that we do in life. With this planetary vision in mind, I hope you find the programs in this book to the point, personally insightful, and just what you're needing.

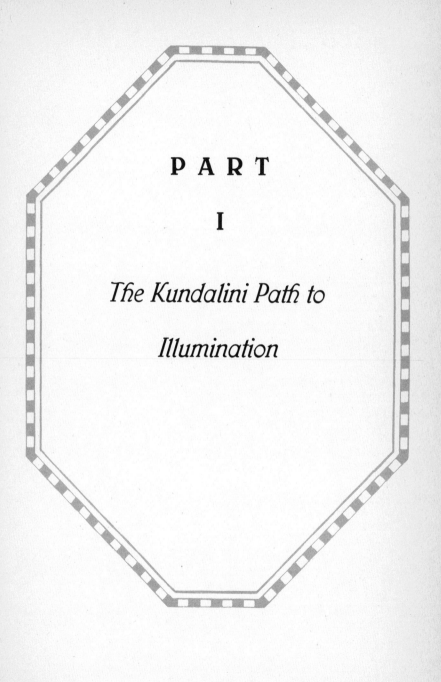

# PART

# I

*The Kundalini Path to*

*Illumination*

# 1

# Coming Alive in the
# Present Moment

*For you to gain* a firsthand understanding of what the kundalini experience is like, you have only to look back into your own childhood, when the lifeforce energy in your body was still comparatively free to express itself spontaneously. Unless you grew up in an especially repressive family environment, you almost certainly entered quite often into a diffuse type of kundalini consciousness, especially when you were engaged in free play.

To recall these moments of childhood bliss, of innocent communion with the divine, is to realize that the kundalini experience, rather than being some vague foreign territory you have no previous knowledge of, is actually the most intimate inner terrain of your personality.

Many times as a child you felt an intense sense of oneness in your heart—a sense of total immersion in the world around you. Perhaps you have maintained in memory the beautiful moments of bliss and pure pleasure you felt, when running wild outside, while gazing at a flower, while laughing and wrestling with a playmate. Can you recall special moments when your body was electric with energy, when your spirit was burning bright with an inner flame, when you felt totally alive, alert, empowered by some magnificent, invisible, infinite source of energy?

You will find as we progress through the programs in this book that childhood memories of spontaneous kundalini experiences will continue to come to you, aiding you in your progress into adult kundalini awakening. These memories offer a reflective view of how energy manifests in the human body.

However, as an adult, with your nervous system now completely developed biologically, the kundalini experience will not be the same as it was when you were a child. During your developmental years and through puberty, your kundalini energy was being directed almost entirely toward nurturing and completing your grand genetic design. Now, as an adult, with the biological phase of your development completed, you are in position to employ your kundalini energies toward more subtle, spiritual dimensions of development.

## Spontaneous Kundalini Upsurges

Even without formal kundalini meditation or meditations by other names that achieve a similar effect, we are all continually evolving spiritually. It's a mistake to think that only people who practice formal meditation are progressing spiritually. One of the true mysteries and blessings of humanity is that our kundalini energy often spontaneously surges up through our various energy centers, encouraging a new awakening into more expansive levels of consciousness.

In every culture, there are various traditional ways that communities allow for stimulating moments of kundalini illumination and release. Dancing, for instance, has always been a part of all human cultures. Through moving totally into rhythm, into breathing, into movement, into our physical presence here in the eternal present moment, we can readily induce a sudden increase in the flow of kundalini energy through our bodies, minds, and souls.

A variation on this theme is the playing of sports. Jogging, for example, recently became an extremely popular way to regularly shift into higher levels of kundalini consciousness. Pleasureful walking with the mind at rest accomplishes the same desired aim.

Traditionally, singing was also a powerful vehicle for transforming one's consciousness and energetic condition quickly into kundalini illumination. Both in the church and the home, groups of people used to sing themselves communally into the kundalini experience.

Another very common way to induce spiritual states of mind has been through the use of concoctions that alter consciousness. Alcohol has been one of the primary vehicles for temporarily increasing the flow of kundalini energy in the body, which in a very limited and distorted way it sometimes does. Hashish and marijuana have also been used throughout the world since time immemorial for temporarily providing a rush of kundalini energy through the nervous system. And definitely, strong psychedelics such as magic mushrooms (psilocybin), peyote (mescaline), and the recently invented LSD all can induce a radical temporary increase in kundalini energization. A great many people have at least temporarily satisfied their spiritual hunger for transcendence by using such drugs. Many report remarkable kundalini experiences. However, the dangers and limitations of such chemically induced initiations into higher states of consciousness are legion.

Another primary way to move into kundalini empowerment and realization has been through the hatha-yoga path of physical postures, as developed for many thousands of years in India, and now quite popular in our culture as well. By consciously holding certain postures that stimulate various glandular secretions in the body, and by quieting the thinking mind through tuning in to the breathing, a deep purification and energization can take place.

Perhaps the main source for regular kundalini energization and temporary illumination has always been, is now, and probably always will be, the human act of sexual intercourse. Because our sexual energy is our most intimate expression of the infinite creative power of the universe, erotic experiences provide us with a direct form of access when we seek a rush of kundalini illumination. Orgasm is our most certain way to interface with the divine.

With all of these ways for accessing kundalini surges of power and pleasure, bliss and self-realization, almost all of us find our own everyday patterns for at least momentarily tapping into a short rush of kundalini presence as we go through each week's routines. Human beings do hunger for transcendence—this is a natural, instinctive, God-given desire. The true challenge of spiritual life is to discover the most effective, satisfying, and rewarding techniques for tapping into increased spiritual energy in our everyday lives.

## CONSCIOUS MEDITATION

Perhaps in an ideal world where emotional inhibitions and mental contractions didn't exist, we would have no need for consciously encouraging our spiritual development through kundalini meditations. If children were taught from birth onward to value and nurture their spiritual dimensions of consciousness, rather than to fear and avoid them, our spiritual development would progress with the same natural certainty as our biological development.

However, as you know from your own childhood, and as I have seen with sometimes upsetting clarity in my work as a psychologist, almost all of us grow up with our minds focused on the material dimensions of life. We receive very little encouragement from our culture to tune in to our spiritual nature, to trust our inner Guide, and to open ourselves to the radical inflow of kundalini energies in everyday life. We live in a society that encourages us to be consumers rather than meditators, that reinforces our ability to work at a boring job all our lives, but discourages our natural desire to explore the vast unknown mystic realms of our being.

However, "culture bashing" is pointless—it does little good to cry over our cultural fate. Life for everyone everywhere always has been and always will be a challenge. We are quite lucky to live during a period of history when we can readily find help in our personal spiritual explorations. It is a true blessing to be able to go to a bookstore or library and immediately find books that teach the ancient, secret techniques for waking ourselves up to our own infinite presence.

What we are actually doing through learning conscious kundalini meditation techniques is simply accelerating the natural process of spiritual awakening, as we gently put aside the psychological hindrances in our personalities that block spiritual illumination. By assuming responsibility for turning our personal attention toward the divine within us, toward the inner Master who will guide us lovingly toward greater and greater union with the infinite divine, we are giving ourselves the ultimate gift of love and liberation.

## NATURAL KUNDALINI BLOCKING MECHANISMS

Although the universe's infinite kundalini energy is available to each of us every moment of our lives, our nervous systems as well as our cultural systems contain definite blocking mechanisms that keep us from being constantly overwhelmed with creative power.

Our biological constitution can realistically be seen as a step-down transformer in which the infinite flow of lifeforce in the universe is filtered and reduced to just the right level to maintain a single human body. If the balance were too high or too low, we would not survive. And since the survival function of the body is primary for the continuation of our species, it makes perfect sense that over the aeons, we have naturally evolved into creatures who limit the kundalini flow in our bodies to functional levels.

Perhaps here we can see the crucial difference between the other creatures that populate this earth and humans—we possess not only the basic kundalini lifeforce that animates all creatures but also the ability to consciously develop our nervous systems so that they can receive more kundalini energy, so as to enhance our deeper levels of consciousness that lie beyond the gross dimensions of physical survival.

Very good reasons remain for honoring and maintaining the genetic blocking devices in our nervous systems that limit the flow of the lifeforce through our bodies and minds. If too much of this energy flows through us too fast, our nervous systems, unprepared, react much like an electrical system that receives too powerful an electrical upsurge. This is the serious danger of uncontrolled kundalini awakening.

As I mentioned briefly already, in this book I am offering a path to kundalini awakening that avoids this "overamping" danger completely. My assumption is that what you are seeking is *not* a path that blasts you out of your normal life and into extreme spiritual states of consciousness that can prove dysfunctional. Instead, what is needed is a potent yet safe approach to opening up to higher levels of kundalini energy.

For most of us there is simply no reasonable possibility of leaving our present situation, even if we wanted to, and devoting our entire lives to the solitary pursuit of our private spiritual awakening. Most of us hunger instead for a meditational life that fits perfectly into our existing routines and habits, but that magically transforms our everyday experiences into a higher level of awareness.

To seek a pragmatic way to enhance our lifeforce so that in everything we do, we have more energy, more pleasure, and more intuitive clarity into the deeper spiritual levels of human existence— this is nothing less than our natural spiritual birthright.

## LOOKING TO THE SOURCE: YOUR OWN SEVEN ENERGY CENTERS

As I mentioned in the Introduction, and as we will explore in depth throughout this book, a series of chakras, or specific energy centers, are located at different positions up and down the human spine. These energy centers are both physiological concentrations of nerve ganglia that control different regions and organs of our physical being, and also energetic spiritual centers, specific vortexes of energy beyond present scientific examination or description.

These energy centers are of course empowered by the basic lifeforce of the universe. When, through meditation of one kind or another, increased kundalini energy is brought up into these energy centers, they become, as Itzhak Bentov says in his book, *Stalking the Wild Pendulum*, "receptors and distributors of inflowing cosmic energy for the body."

In the same way that physics shows us that everything is constantly vibrating back and forth between matter and energy, as Einstein envisioned, kundalini meditation shows us directly that our physical energy centers vibrate constantly into their parallel energetic forms, and back again—they are both physical and energetic, as is all of creation.

The ancient Yogic Masters discovered through direct perceptual investigation of their own inner realities that in the human body there are seven such energetic vortexes, which correspond to the seven main groupings of nerve ganglia up and down the spine. These energetic vortexes are not separate esoteric entities as they are sometimes portrayed but instead are the nervous system's higher-level centers of organization and control, directing all the supposedly mundane functionings of the body and mind. Our thoughts, our diet, our physical activity or lack of it, our emotions, and also our spiritual meditative routines all influence our energetic centers, and are strongly influenced by them in turn.

Let me speak at this point in more depth about the primary qualities of each of the seven chakras that at this very moment are actively present in your own body, reflecting your present state of development toward ultimate union with your divine nature. I will begin with general insights into the nature of the chakras, and as the book progresses we will refine our understanding to include the more subtle explanations of chakra functioning. Please hold in mind that these beginning descriptions only aim us in the general direction of understanding the interrelated functioning of the energy centers. Only by tuning directly in to the experience of your own particular chakras will you gain true personal insight into their nature.

## The First Chakra

Often called the "Earth Chakra," the first chakra lies at the base of your spine and is the energetic gateway between the organic world of Mother Earth beneath you and the mental and spiritual worlds that can be awakened step-by-step up your spine.

This chakra strongly connects you to your childhood past and to the entire outside world of physical phenomenon. It therefore is of vital importance in your life. This chakra energized your physical development up through puberty, and maintains your basic sense of physical contact with the planet.

Through meditating on this chakra, as you will learn to do in this book, you help yourself become more grounded, more solid and powerful at physical levels of survival. First-chakra meditation is also very important if you have health problems. Furthermore, this chakra underlies your ability to go out and be a success in the everyday world around you.

The "Earth Chakra" should be seen as the foundation for everything else that will come to you when working with the higher chakras. The Kundalini Goddess is said to lie coiled three and a half times around this chakra. Only by lovingly focusing on this beginning energetic base can kundalini energy be consciously tapped and sent upward through all the other energy centers.

## The Second Chakra

The second, or "Sexual Chakra," located in the sexual organs, becomes activated once the work of the first chakra is completed at puberty. Through the awakening of this chakra you move from being a creation of your parents to becoming a creative being who in turn creates the new generation. As Joseph Chilton Pearce states so succinctly in *Magical Child Matures*, "The physical system (the first chakra) is the support system for sexuality (the second chakra), and sexuality is the support system for further development of kundalini (the higher chakras)."

By doing second-chakra meditations, you will increase your sexual charge and bring a spiritual vitality to your erotic feelings and interactions. At the same time, you will feel this raw procreative energy being transmuted into a more pure vibration that can rise up and permeate your other chakras and also flow down to energize your first-chakra survival powers. There is also great purification and cleansing power in this chakra, especially related to imbalances in your emotional personality.

## The Third Chakra

Called the "Power Chakra," the third chakra is associated with fire, with combustion, with anger, joy, and laughter. It is located between the navel and the solar plexus in the body and is said to generate a mythical fire in the belly. It is the energy of the solar system radiating in our personal lives, and like the sun, creates energy for us to burn.

This chakra strongly influences the adrenal glands. By learning to balance the energy in this chakra you will bring your physical and emotional condition to a point of moderation. Your heartbeat will become even and calm. Your raw willpower will become especially transformed into a higher quality of spiritual presence in the world. In Western terms, the Holy Spirit can be employed to transform your raw willpower so that your actions harmonize with the will of the Spirit instead of your ego-centered will.

Many traditions, such as those of the Yaqui Indians, the Zen Buddhists, and the martial-arts disciplines, focus a great deal on this third chakra, since it is the center of raw, uncommitted willpower. Whether we send this energy down into brute sexuality and worldly dominance, or up into the heart to be used for personal transformation, determines if we use this energy in malevolent or positive ways.

As we will see later, empowering the third chakra through kundalini meditations is especially powerful because it awakens our contact with the sun—the masculine fire-energy of the universe. When this potent surge of energy is merged with both the lower, grounded chakras and the higher, love-dominated chakras, our whole experience of life becomes transformed.

### The Fourth Chakra

The "Heart Chakra," located in the center of the chest, is the guiding light that shows the third chakra how to burn its raw energy in loving ways, shows the second chakra how to manifest its sexual energy through the transmutation of love, and shows the first chakra how to merge the physical with the divine.

The Heart Chakra is equidistant between the first and the seventh chakra, between earth and heaven. It is the centerpoint of the primary emotional energy of the universe, which we call love. It balances the chakras above with the chakras below, all of equal importance.

Although in Yogic tradition, and in Christian tradition as well, "the above" has often been valued higher than "the below," it seems that, as ecologically minded human beings, we must put aside this prejudice of the past against the lower chakras if we are to value this earth of ours as much as we value the heaven above us. A great deal of terrible damage has been done to our planet because of our religious prejudice against the lower chakras. We must value a balance of all the chakras as equal energetic presences, rather than always striving to leave the lower and rise up to the higher.

As mentioned before, my approach to chakra balancing, as taught to me by my main teachers, is to make the Heart Chakra central, and excursions into the realms of spirit (above) and matter (below) always in conjunction with the heart. This for me makes kundalini meditation ecologically sound as well as energetically safe.

Love, the primary quality of the fourth chakra, is, as Jesus taught, God manifest in human life: "God is Love." If the fourth chakra is where love is to be found, we spontaneously know where to place the center of our kundalini explorations, and how to avoid extremes that throw us off center spiritually. With the fourth energy center we have reached the natural centerpoint of kundalini meditation.

The fourth chakra strongly influences the functioning of the thymus gland, located in the center of the chest just behind the upper breastbone. Because this gland directly influences the functioning of our immune system, fourth-chakra balancing and energization can also have a profound effect on our overall health and resistance to disease.

## The Fifth Chakra

The fifth chakra, often called the "Communication Chakra," is located in our throat region—in our larynx and thyroid gland from a physical point of view. This is the center of communication, of talking, of expressing our inner depths of feeling in words that the people around us can understand.

Vocalization is one of the main vehicles for kundalini awakening, as we will see in detail later on. When I speak of chanting, I speak of activating this fifth chakra and using it to empower the other chakras.

In our everyday lives, this chakra is our vehicle for spreading our spiritual realizations to the world around us. This is where we begin to listen to ourselves and realize what we are saying.

The fifth chakra is also the center for dreaming and imagination activity, and sometimes for what are called out-of-the-body experiences as well. This chakra stimulates and integrates conceptual realization of spiritual insights. It is the bridge between feeling and thinking, between the concrete and the abstract. Spiritual visions emanate from this chakra, sometimes in great glory and infinite detail.

This fifth energy center is often overly stimulated in our culture, even without the supposedly lower chakras being energized. When this happens, a person is fixated on the conceptual mode of the mind without adequate heart resonance to balance intellect with love. Meditation on this chakra is equally important for those of us who are overly intellectual and those of us who have yet to tap into our intellectual, verbal powers.

The gland controlled by the fifth chakra is the thyroid and parathyroid, which of course affects the entire nervous system, metabolism, and muscular control. If this gland is out of balance, people tend to have chronic colds and sore throats, stiff necks, and later in life, hearing problems. Balancing this chakra will help relieve these conditions at the same time that it opens kundalini energy to flow up and down into the other chakras.

## The Sixth Chakra

The "Intuitive Chakra" is the chakra you find right between and above your eyes. It is traditionally referred to as "The Third Eye." This is the seat of true wisdom, where your thinking mind comes into contact with your intuitive mind. This is where, if you are listening during meditation, God speaks to you directly.

The great living spiritual Master Gurumayi of Ganeshpuri urges us to maintain a primary focus on the Heart Chakra while activating the sixth chakra, so that love is always the primary foundation of insight. In this way we can be, as Jesus suggested, "in the world but not of it," balanced perfectly between biological and spiritual in all our dealings with the world around us. We will certainly adhere to this wisdom in our kundalini meditations in this book.

The sixth chakra influences the pituitary gland in the brain, and thus determines the entire functioning of the body and mind at high levels. By bringing energy up and down into this center, you can alleviate many depressive patterns and balance the nervous system to help overcome paranoia and distorted perceptions of reality. At lesser levels, headaches can be left behind through energetic balancing of this chakra, as well as nightmares and many visual problems. This chakra is where spiritual balancing heals emotional distortions.

### The Seventh Chakra

Also called the "Crown Chakra," the seventh chakra, which is located at the top of the head, is light years beyond the lower chakras. The true nature of the seventh chakra is beyond human comprehension. The advice of all my teachers on the kundalini path, and mine to you as well, is not to ever try to push yourself into seventh-chakra consciousness. This experience will come to you when your nervous system is fully prepared for such infinite realization and union with the creative force of the universe.

However, in regular kundalini meditation, it is important to focus your attention for at least short periods directly to this center so that your energetic system can balance itself and you can open yourself to the inflow of energy from above. There should be no inhibition regarding direct focusing on the seventh chakra. As long as you don't use special techniques for overstimulating this chakra, a regular and quite natural inflow of white-light energy and insight can be received.

The seventh chakra controls the pineal gland in the brain.

Medicine claims that this mysterious gland is defunct. But Yogis for thousands of years have come to know intimately from the inside out that the pineal gland is awakened through kundalini energy and begins secreting only when we become spiritually awakened. In fact, biochemically, it is possible to talk about enlightenment as a state where the pineal gland is regularly secreting special hormones into the body's lower glandular system.

In more spiritual terms, to regularly include the seventh chakra in our kundalini balancing meditations is to welcome the universal Holy Spirit to flow downward into our physical and energetic bodies, and to flood our lives with the ultimate healing and inspirational power of the universe.


Let me give you a breather at this point, which will allow you to put the book aside at least for a few good breaths, and turn your attention to your own spine and brain where these energy centers are located. It will, of course, take time for you to learn how to make deep experiential contact with these chakra centers. The purpose of this book is to help you learn to direct your attention so that you discover for yourself the presence of these energetic centers in your body. The spiritual challenge is to go beyond mental concepts of chakras and energy centers and kundalini upflows and all the rest, and to encounter these realities directly.

Right now, without making any effort, see what experience comes to you if you close your eyes after reading this paragraph . . . tune in to your breaths as they come and go . . . and look one after the other in the general direction of each of the seven chakras we just discussed. . . .

## KUNDALINI AND ECOLOGICAL CONSCIOUSNESS

You now have a rough image of the seven different energy centers in your body, and the purpose and value of kundalini meditation. Our challenge in this book is to learn to focus your attention powerfully on each of your chakras in turn, and also to develop the expanded state of consciousness where you are aware of all seven chakras at once, so that you become a whole, integrated spiritual energy system. Through such meditating you will regularly bring yourself into optimum position for rapid spiritual advancement, not just for your own benefit, but for those around you.

Gopi Krishna said in his book *Kundalini for the New Age*, "Kundalini is the divine mechanism for the transformation of the whole race from an aimless crowd of jostling, fighting people into a harmonious assembly of illuminated beings." As you know, we are at a point in human history where we are standing with our spiritual backs against the ecological wall. If we don't act to expand our spiritual intelligence and channel more love and wisdom into our environment, we might very quickly destroy human civilization as we know it.

There is much talk these days about our being in danger of destroying our fragile planet through our antiecological actions. However, as Dr. Lewis Thomas has pointed out in *The Lives of a Cell*, "It is an illusion to think that there is anything fragile about the life of the earth. Surely this is the toughest membrane imaginable in the universe. We are the delicate part, transient and vulnerable."

Our striving for higher consciousness through kundalini awakening is not to save the planet itself, but to preserve the more delicate species, including our extremely delicate human culture that exists so precariously at the top of the life chain. Along with the magnificent whale and dolphin populations, we humans seem to be the vanguard of consciousness here on planet Earth. Our challenge is to accelerate the evolution of human spiritual awareness into more humane dimensions, rather than perpetuating lower levels of consciousness.

We are in many ways the eyes and ears of God. We have an inherent responsibility to refine our spiritual senses so that we perceive reality clearly and act accordingly. Kundalini awakening from my point of view is not a solitary pursuit done purely for selfish reasons. On the contrary, kundalini meditation is an act of communal intent, as we personally awaken our internal contact with our spiritual essence and let this spiritual power flow outward through our actions to the benefit of all of humankind. Infinite energy is available in the universe, as the new physics shows us. Our challenge as human beings is to learn how to participate in this lifeforce energy in safe yet powerful ways.

These are big words, and they need to be balanced with pragmatic programs that in fact offer access to this heightened level of human consciousness. Let me explain clearly at this point the approach we are going to use in this book for realizing both our ecological and spiritual desires.

## APPROACHING MEDITATION

In Part II of this book, which is the practical heart of the program for kundalini awakening, I will walk you chapter by chapter through a complete meditation program for each chakra. You will learn to focus on and activate whatever energy centers you feel need extra loving attention each time you sit down to do a meditation session. More important, you will develop the ability to balance all seven of the chakras into a harmonious whole, so that your entire life is vibrant and in balance with your spiritual center.

Meditation sessions can be from seven breaths to seven hours long, or anywhere in between. I will offer several different meditations for each chakra so that you can choose which one suits your situation when you have time to meditate. I will also teach you how to do chakra meditations even when you are busy doing something else. Kundalini meditation should become a constant state of mind and spirit.

My basic suggestion is that you do try to set aside one regular time period each day for kundalini meditation, so that you have a definite meditative discipline in your life. This is a very important goal.

I will also teach you how to meditate for shorter periods of time, no matter where you might be or what you might be doing. Spontaneous meditations are also key to spiritual growth, where you open yourself to insight and realization right when it is ready to come flooding into you.

We are constantly, every moment of every day, in the process of waking up to new realms of consciousness. Spiritual growth is an infinite process. If we devote time regularly to conscious awakening, and open to it whenever it strikes us, we can enjoy every step along the way!


## BREATH AWARENESS:
## THE FIRST VEHICLE IN ACTION

At this point, I want to teach you a primary meditation, one that will underlie all the rest of the meditations you will learn in this program. This meditation focuses on the first "vehicle" I spoke of earlier—breath awareness. My main teacher, Thakin Kung, placed the highest value on this seemingly simple meditation.

You breathe continuously throughout your lifetime. To breathe is to live. To stop breathing is to die. Our first and last breaths on planet Earth are the bookends of our time spent here.

But most of us are usually unconscious of our moment-to-moment breathing. Our minds get so busy thinking about the past and the future, making plans, worrying, dreaming, and so on and so forth, that we very easily lose awareness of our present-moment experience.

Breath meditation serves to bring us immediately back into the eternal present moment. By regularly observing our inhales and exhales, we tune our awareness in to the vital realm of consciousness that is alive in the here and now.

All true spiritual teachings emphasize that the only place we will ever find God is right here, right now, in our unfolding present moment. God is to be found neither in the past nor in the future. The past and the future are after all nothing but mental extensions of the infinite, eternal present—as mystics have been telling us for thousands of years.

Therefore, all true spiritual teachings naturally begin by helping students move into present-moment consciousness. This is done by learning ways to let go of the mind's chronic habits of drifting off into concepts, fantasies, and memories.

Some meditative techniques employ "karate" attacks on the thinking mind, in order to kill off the ego and silence the personal flow of words through consciousness. I greatly prefer to use "judo" instead. We don't have to become hostile or negative toward the thinking mind in order to silence its chronic thought-flows.

The great trick in quieting the thinking mind is to give it something worthwhile to do—a challenging task which directly aids in the process of focusing our attention fully on the present moment. Breath meditation does exactly this, when approached properly. It puts the thinking mind to work at an essential spiritual job—that of conscientiously observing each inhale and exhale as breathing unfolds in the present moment.

## The Breath-Anchor Meditation

Let me give you the basic breath-awareness process, which you can begin to master step-by-step in the weeks to come.

(1) Without making any effort to alter or control your breathing, simply tune in to the actual physical sensations you feel in your nose as air rushes in and out the nostrils with every new breath. . . . Be sure to consciously relax your tongue and jaw. . . .

(2) At the same time, tune in to the sounds created by the air rushing in and out of your nose as you continue breathing. . . .

(3) Right in the middle of your awareness of air rushing in and out of your nose, expand your awareness to also include the sensations of physical movement in your chest and belly as you breathe. . . .

(4) As you remain aware of these breathing experiences, allow your awareness to expand to include the tip of your nose . . . your hands and fingers . . . your feet and toes . . . your whole body here in the present moment. . . . Relax and enjoy the pure experience of effortless breathing and meditative calm. . . .

# 2

# Direct Contact with
# the Divine

*Kundalini meditation, along with* all other meditative traditions of the world, has as its underlying goal the expansion of human consciousness. In this chapter we're going to explore precisely what is meant by the term "consciousness expansion," and also learn a simple yet extremely potent consciousness-expansion meditation that shows first-hand the process that leads to spiritual illumination.

I have always liked the description of enlightenment offered by Thaddeus Golas in his magical book, *The Lazy Man's Guide to Enlightenment.* He says, "Enlightenment is any experience of expanding our consciousness beyond its present limits. Perfect enlightenment is realizing that we have no limits at all—and that the entire universe is alive."

To be "conscious" means simply to be aware of what is happening in the present moment, to hold our attention here, and recognize what we are perceiving. "Consciousness expansion" means being aware of more of reality than we normally are.

At the end of the first chapter, you experienced for yourself the basic consciousness-expanding exercise of turning your attention more and more completely to your breathing, and remaining aware of whatever experiences come to you. Each time you do that meditation (I suggest doing it at least four times a day) you'll have a completely new experience—because no one ever breathes the same breath more than once. We never feel the same way twice. It's always new! There are no limits to the expansive experiences that come to us when we turn our attention to our breathing and observe what is happening in the present moment.

In sum, the expansion of consciousness requires simply that we stay in tune with whatever is coming into existence in the present moment—and that we remain open to letting go of old concepts and anticipations that are not in harmony with the newly emerging reality being formed around us in each new moment.

## ONENESS WITH OUR OWN CONSCIOUSNESS

Itzhak Bentov formally defines consciousness as "the capacity of a system to respond to stimuli." I like this definition because it shows that human consciousness is not an isolated entity, but rather an interactive participant in what is being experienced.

As we'll see step-by-step, every time you turn your attention to your breathing, and furthermore to your energy centers, an instant interaction takes place between the habitual functioning of these aspects of your body and your present level of consciousness. Thus, when you focus your attention on your chakras, when you expand your awareness to include these centers of energetic activity, your mind's attention immediately becomes an active agent in the functioning of these chakra centers. This is what makes meditation powerful.

Scientists at the turn of the century finally began to realize that it is impossible to perform an objective experiment—because the experimenter's consciousness is always interacting with the experiment and influencing the results. This has been a radical realization for scientists to come to terms with. But from a spiritual point of view, the same realization is blatantly obvious, and has been taught for many thousands of years by the great Yogis of the East. There is no separating the power of consciousness from what it is focusing upon.

## EXPANSIONS AND CONTRACTIONS OF AWARENESS

As I'm sure you know from your own observations, any particular event that happens on the face of this earth can be experienced in thousands of different ways, depending on the state of consciousness of the individual. People in an earthly paradise can experience it as hell if their inner reality is contracted and in pain. Conversely, it is quite possible to be in an absolutely hellish situation and expand into a blissful experience anyway.

One of our truly primal freedoms, perhaps the only true freedom, is our ability to determine where we are going to focus our attention at any given moment—and whether we are going to expand our consciousness or contract it.

It's important to see clearly that consciousness is not a quality that simply continues to expand more and more through our lives. Consciousness is instead continually expanding and contracting, moment to moment. We can be beautifully expansive, carried away with blissful feelings and insights; then something can happen to drop us down to a terrible level of contraction.

What we are aiming toward through kundalini-awakening meditations is more conscious control over the expansions and contractions of our everyday awareness. In the process of growing up, we inherited from our parents and community certain habitual patterns of consciousness. The challenge of a spiritually evolving person is to gain an expanded perception of these habitual patterns of consciousness so that they can be evaluated, and if found to inhibit our present potential for consciousness expansion, purposely let go of.

As an example, consider your conditioned breathing habits. Certain things that happen to you tend to make your breathing contract. If you see two men fighting as you come around a corner, for instance, your breathing will tense and contract. Conversely, if you see a beautiful sunset, your breathing will almost certainly relax and expand.

These reactions happen reflexively, based on past conditioning. In a very real way, we are all prisoners of our old programmings, because they determine when our consciousness expands and when it contracts.

But if we begin to be aware of how our breathing reacts automatically to different situations, we can consciously begin to overcome those habits and gain a new sense of freedom in our lives. Kundalini meditation serves this vital beginning function of helping us to see how we habitually react and contract in life situations. And in the process of seeing ourselves clearly, we move into position to let go of old reactions, and open up to more expansive responses to life.

## FEAR: THE PRIMARY CONTRACTION AGENT

A basic psychological fact is that consciousness contracts in fear, and relaxes and expands in peace. When we feel threatened by something, we shut it out, we close down our awareness. When we feel secure and receptive, we expand.

One day recently, my little boy and I were watching a lowly slug making its way across the garden path. I explained to him that a slug has a certain level of consciousness, which determines its actions. For instance, it expands its antennas and moves around in its environment when it senses no danger. But as soon as it feels threatened, it contracts, pulls back its antennas, and basically goes unconscious to avoid danger. We tend to do the same thing.

Fear is the great enemy of spiritual growth. And there must be a certain sense of faith within us, if we are to risk expanding our consciousness in spiritual directions. Joseph Chilton Pearce speaks of how faith plays a vital function in chakra awakening, and I certainly agree. If we don't deep down trust in the spiritual universe, if we don't make contact with our inner Master and feel we are being guided in positive directions, then we won't be able to open ourselves to kundalini awakening—because who knows what we might encounter as we let go of the known past and venture into genuinely new territory within us.

We tend as a culture to place our trust in material things, in technological powers, and to remain afraid of our inner spiritual presence and power. This underlying fear of our spiritual dynamics is what keeps most of us unaware that we possess these energetic centers up and down our spines.

The suggestion of this book is that we look for ourselves to see if the energetic presence of our chakra systems is anything to fear. Only when we overcome cultural conditionings that keep us in contraction against spiritual illumination, can we activate our energy centers and raise ourselves into new heights of spiritual consciousness.

## MEDITATING WHILE READING

There is a special way to approach the act of reading which instantly turns the usually mundane experience of reading into a deep meditation. I offer you this as a spiritual challenge for the rest of this book, and beyond.

The process is quite simple. As the words, paragraphs, and pages go by, see to what extent you can stay aware of your breathing, of the experience of each new inhale and exhale as you read. Expand your consciousness so that you are aware of your whole body here in the present moment, while at the same time taking in the ongoing flow of words.

This way of "breathing yourself" through the reading experience is really not so difficult, and it turns reading into a meditational path in itself. I myself first heard of this "reading-as-meditation" suggestion from the great contemporary Indian spiritual teacher

Krishnamurti some twenty years ago—when a small group of us were gathered at his home in Ojai, California. Ever since, I have been living within the magic of the suggestion. I'm pleased to pass it on to you for your future reading pleasure.

Let me guide you through this basic process a little more, so you can come fully into this new meditative state of reading. As you continue reading these words, simply slow down your reading pace a bit, relax, and tune in to your breathing while you continue to read. . . . Feel the air rushing in and out your nose as you read these words. . . . Enjoy being aware of your own self, even while you are reading the words on this page. . . . Let your consciousness expand effortlessly so that you are reading and breathing at the same time. . . . While you remain aware of the air flowing in and out your nose, allow your consciousness to expand so that you are also aware of the movements in your chest and belly caused by each new breath. . . . Hold in mind that breathing is the beginning and ending of kundalini awakening. . . . To remain fully aware of your breathing right in the midst of whatever you might be doing—this is true enlightenment itself. . . .


## BREATH AND HEART TOGETHER

Kundalini meditation follows the natural path of human consciousness-expansion. First, we tune in to the vital bodily function of breathing. Then comes an expansion of consciousness to include both the breath experience and the heart experience at the same time.

I first learned this meditative process from Alan Watts in San Francisco in 1969. One day he guided me through the basic breath-awareness meditation I just taught you, which is a classic in Zen Buddhist contemplation. Then he said, "Let your awareness of your breathing expand effortlessly so that, right in the middle of your breathing, you experience your heartbeat or pulse at the same time."

## The Breath-Heart Meditation

Let me give you space now to pause and practice this breath-heart meditation in action. After reading this paragraph, put the book aside. . . . Get up and jump a bit if you want to get your heart beating more vigorously before doing the meditation . . . then sit quietly . . . close your eyes perhaps . . . tune in to your breathing . . . feel the air rushing in and out your nose. . . . At the same time, experience the sensations of movement in your chest and belly as you breathe . . . and feel your heartbeat or pulse happening right in the middle of your breathing experience. . . .

Some people initially find it a bit difficult to tune in to their heartbeat in the middle of their breathing. Keep in mind that mastering the meditations I am teaching you takes time and patience. You are not expected to master such primal expansions in a sitting, in a week, even in a month or year. I've been exploring these basic expansions for twenty-some years now, and every time I do them, the experience is still radical, unexpected—a new vision into the infinite realms of consciousness.

## WHOLE-BODY AWAKENING

We have now tuned in to the constant life-giving happenings of breathing and heartbeat, which let us know that we are alive here in the eternal present moment. We have fine-tuned our mind's attention to the air around us that we are taking into our lungs, and felt the pumping power of our hearts as oxygen is circulated throughout every artery and capillary of our body. Through this focusing of our mind's attention inward, we have brought our awareness into an expanded interface with every cell in our body that receives oxygen in the circulatory system. To feel our pulse throughout the body is truly to expand consciousness to include the whole of our physical being.

Now we come to the final expansion in this "coming-alive-in-the-present-moment" meditation. This is to expand your awareness to include your breathing, your heartbeat, and at the same time, your sense of balance within the earth's force field of gravity.

Every muscle in your body is right now maintaining a particular level of tension or relaxation, to keep you upright as you read this book. To tune in to your moment-to-moment experience of balance is realistically to expand your awareness to include every muscle in your body that participates in the balancing process. By becoming aware of the ongoing process of balancing, you become aware of all the muscles in your body at once, and all your skeletal bones as well.

Again, let me guide you effortlessly through this consciousness-expansion process. Even while reading these words, you can feel the process happening, and hopefully, you will set aside a few minutes every hour to practice this meditation on your own, so that you establish a deep habit of mind that guides you through the expansion process regularly, every new day of your new life.

Turn your attention to:

(1) The air rushing in and out your nose . . .
(2) The movements in your chest and belly now as you breathe . . .
(3) Your heartbeat or pulse right in the middle of your breathing experience . . .
(4) Your sense of balance as gravity pulls on your body and your muscles respond with perfect precision to keep you upright. . . .

## THE WHOLE-BODY EXPANSION MEDITATION

With this four-step meditation, you now know the essential process for bringing yourself into the eternal present moment, where all spiritual exploration takes place. Nothing of significance can come on deeper planes of consciousness unless you first bring yourself fully into this awareness of your own presence.

This primary expansion meditation will be used to begin each kundalini session of this book. I suggest that you commit this progression of consciousness expansion to memory—that you learn it by heart before going further in this book. Only to the extent that you are aware of yourself as a whole, unified entity can you be experientially cognizant of your individual chakras and their influence in your life.

Let me state clearly what this whole-body expansion meditation consists of:

(1) Awareness of the actual sensation of the air rushing in and out your nose with every new breath. . . .

(2) The expansion of awareness to also include the movements in your chest and belly as you breathe. . . .

(3) The further effortless expansion of awareness to include your heartbeat or pulse in your body. . . .

(4) The expansion of consciousness to also include your muscular sense of balance in the present moment. . . .

I have just given you a primary key to kundalini awakening—your ability to consciously expand your usual consciousness to include your whole body, here in the present moment. Your challenge is to begin to practice this four-step meditation often, once an hour if you can remember to, so that a new spiritual habit of awareness begins to take root inside you, which will step-by-step blossom into full kundalini illumination.

This beginning meditation is the turning on of the light through which you will be able to see the deeper spiritual realities of your own existence. Always remember: turn on the light—tune in to your full presence here in the present moment—before doing any of the more advanced chakra meditations.

## MEET YOUR CHAKRAS

Once you move through the four-step preliminary meditation just outlined, you are in position to expand your mind's attention another crucial notch to include the specific locations in your body where kundalini energy stimulates chakra activity.

We have discussed already at a conceptual level where the seven chakras are found in your body. For the rest of this chapter—and for the rest of your life if you remain a dedicated kundalini meditator— we are going to explore these chakras experientially.

There are several chakras that are usually relatively easy to turn your experiential consciousness toward. For instance, if I say "be aware of your Heart Chakra," you will probably have a fairly good idea where to look with your inner awareness. Likewise with the Sexual Chakra—the general location is fairly well known. Let me guide you through a preliminary experiential exploration of your seven chakras so you can see how well your mind focuses your power of attention in each of the seven directions.

**Chakra One:** First, relax, be aware of your breathing, your heart-beat, your balance here in the present moment . . . and in this expanded state of awareness, turn your power of attention to the bottom of your spine, where your body meets the earth in the sitting position. . . .

**Chakra Two:** Now while you remain aware of your breathing and whole-body presence, move your awareness up to your sexual center, to your genital region. . . .

**Chakra Three:** Now shift your awareness up into your belly, to your third chakra's power center. . . .

**Chakra Four:** Now move your awareness effortlessly up into your Heart Chakra, found in the center of your chest. . . .

**Chakra Five:** Now shift your awareness up into your throat, into the Communications Chakra. . . .

**Chakra Six:** Now effortlessly allow your awareness to move up to the point between your eyes deep within your brain, where your intuitive, sixth chakra is located. . . .

**Chakra Seven:** And now move your awareness up to the top of your head, to the seventh, Crown Chakra. . . .

## THE PRAGMATICS OF KUNDALINI AWAKENING

If you opened yourself to the experience I just guided you through, you just performed the essence of kundalini meditation. While aware of your whole-body presence, you focused on each of the seven energy centers in your body. Each of you will have had a different beginning experience with each chakra, based on many factors from your past and your basic makeup as an individual. But you all experienced the seven primary building blocks of human existence.

Remember to be as nonjudgmental as possible of your initial ability or inability to make contact with each of the particular chakras. For many of you, some of the chakras will prove quite difficult to focus on at first. This is perfectly natural and to be expected. Full kundalini awakening takes time, of this there is no doubt. As I mentioned, it is optimally a progressive affair, not a sudden overpowering encounter.

Your challenge is to regularly turn your conscious attention in the general direction of each of the seven chakras, so that regardless of your beginning blocks and seeming blindness, you gently bring your conscious mind into contact with the vibratory presence of all seven energy centers in your body.

Let me give you a bit of free time at this point in our discussion so that you can put the book aside if you want to after reading this paragraph and, step-by-step, tune in to your breathing and whole body. Then in serial order, starting with your first chakra and moving step-by-step up through the others, see what your present experience is of each of these energy centers. Here is a list if you are still uncertain as to the order of the chakras:

(1) Earth Chakra at the base of your spine.
(2) Sex Chakra in the reproductive organs.
(3) Power Chakra between the navel and solar plexus.
(4) Heart Chakra in the center of the chest.
(5) Throat Chakra in and around the larynx.
(6) Intuitive Chakra between the eyebrows.
(7) Mystic Chakra at the top of the head.

## CHAKRA FIXATIONS

Ann Ree Colton, a contemporary mystic and teacher of the kundalini path, says in her book *Kundalini West* that "kundalini is an attention-vehicle; where the attention is, there kundalini goes." Most of us habitually limit our attention in general, and hold that attention chronically fixated on just a couple of the energy centers in the body, and thus create a kundalini imbalance in our systems.

The most common imbalances resulting from attention fixation are as follows. Your experience with people around you should corroborate my statements.

A great many of us find ourselves stuck down in the Earth Chakra, still trying to work through adolescent hang-ups and basic survival fears. Instead of advancing beyond childhood phases of development, we flounder in childish feelings and thoughts. For instance, many of us are continually hungering for a mommy to give us everything we need, especially emotionally—instead of moving forward in life and learning to become givers ourselves.

Many of us are overfixated on the second chakra, the sexual center. We crave the pleasure of sexual discharge—we are addicts to stimuli that charge us for yet another genital release. Our culture reinforces this sexual hang-up to an almost pathological level through the media and advertisements. Sex for its own selfish sake has become a hallmark of our present era.

The third chakra is also abused a great deal, by people who chronically play power games, focusing their attention on their raw talent to dominate other people and Mother Nature. It is said by contemporary chakra experts that our present civilization as a whole is caught up in the third chakra, struggling to finally move beyond manipulation and into heartfelt, fourth-chakra participation in the ecological and spiritual realms of consciousness. People fixated on using magic for manipulative purposes are likewise abusing third-chakra energy.

The Heart Chakra might seem one that no one abuses through overfixation. But in fact many people were brought up to be selfless loving creatures. They are chronically giving their love overmuch in the wrong directions and draining themselves through this unwise and imbalanced expression of their capacity to love. We can hide away from taking responsibility for our third-chakra power, for instance, by being overly heart-fixated.

Many of us also fixate on the fifth, Throat Chakra, by thinking and talking all the time, spouting off at the mouth as a chronic habit that drains us and those around us instead of enlightening us. The Throat Chakra is also the center for dreaming and fantasy, and certainly many of us are stuck in this habit of living in a fantasy world instead of tuning in to the realities that beg our attention on planet Earth. Furthermore, people who are chronic head-trippers, who are lost in conceptual thought most of the time, are fixated in this chakra.

It would seem that the sixth chakra, and the seventh as well, would not be available for abuse and misuse. However, there are certain advanced spiritual teachers who remain overly fixated in the sixth chakra of pure intelligence and intuitive wisdom, to the detriment of their full energy system.

Ideally, there should be a steady, even flow of energy through all of the chakras, not favoring nor avoiding any particular one. Any imbalance in one of the chakras will create an imbalance in the others.

It is important that you begin an honest reflection on your own habits of attention. Where along the spine do you habitually fixate your attention? Are you someone down in your sexual regions most of the time, or up in your head? Are you caught up in power plays that keep you down in the third chakra?

Pause again, put the book aside if you want to after reading this paragraph, and reflect on this deep question of which energy centers you habitually fixate on, and which ones you almost never focus your attention on. . . .

## DIRECTION OF KUNDALINI ENERGY FLOWS

Usually, when people first begin to reflect upon kundalini energy flows, they try to visualize energy that rises up from the base of the spine and moves progressively through the chakras until it flashes into the infinite spiritual realms of the seventh chakra. This was my own first impression of kundalini.

The experiential truth of energy flows in the body is this: The lifeforce energy flows both up from the earth through our bodies and also down through the seventh chakra into our bodies from above.

It is essential to understand that our human bodies are receptors of energy both from above and from below. We are in physical form the marriage of heaven and earth, in this important and ultimate energetic sense.

Notice that at the very centerpoint of this marriage of heaven and earth, we find the fourth chakra, the Heart Chakra. A perfect balance between above and below is thus programmed inherently into our nervous systems. When our chakra system is functioning ideally, the energetic upflows and downflows merge with great power and illumination in the central vortex of love. This is our aim.

## A FULLY INTEGRATED ENERGETIC CIRCUIT

When you turn your attention to your chakra system, please keep in mind that you are not going to experience static chakras, each of them existing in and of themselves. You are only going to encounter your chakras as living, energetic centers constantly being activated by energy flowing from both above and below. Chakras exist only in energetic action.

They also exist only in relationship with each other, and with the energetic flows around the body. We speak of separate chakras, but in reality, they are inseparable. Remove one of them from the nervous system and you have a defunct, dead system.

This is why I began this kundalini program by having you focus not on individual chakras but on your whole body. This is why I strongly suggest that every time you begin a chakra meditation, you first go through the basic breath/whole-body meditation so that you are whole in your consciousness before you begin to focus your attention to specific chakras.

This is also why I am offering you maximum direct experiential contact with your chakras, rather than focusing overmuch on the theories and visual concepts of the chakras. As my teacher Thakin Kung suggested, first make contact with the energy itself, with your personal kundalini presence—then occasionally reflect on conceptual structures that make verbal sense of the chakra reality. We do

# Whole-Body Chakra Meditation

With this premise in mind, let's end this chapter by giving you a new opportunity to explore the primary chakra experience, in which you turn your power of attention directly toward your whole energetic system:

(1) Sit quietly, either in a chair with feet on the ground and spine upright, or on the floor on a pillow . . . let your eyes close when they want to, and open when they want to, spontaneously . . . relax your tongue and jaw. . . .

(2) Tune in to your breathing as you learned to earlier in this book, so that your attention comes alive in the present-moment reality of every new inhale and exhale. . . .

(3) Expand your awareness to include your heartbeat or pulse in your body. . . .

(4) Expand your awareness to include your sense of muscular balance within the force field of Mother Earth's gravity. . . .

(5) Expand your awareness effortlessly to include your whole body at once, here in the present moment. . . .

(6) Now, while remaining aware of your whole-body presence, expand your awareness to focus on each of the chakras in turn, allowing two to six breaths for each chakra. . . .

(7) Now let go of individual chakra-focusing and be aware of all the chakras together as one energy system. Open yourself to whatever energy flows you find happening within and around you. . . .

need to feed our thinking, fifth-chakra heads with enough left-brain information to create a mental framework regarding kundalini awakening. But we must maintain a healthy balance between this chakra activity and all the other chakra functions, as we will see in detail later on.

# 3

# Energy Flows and
# Enlightenment

*We can employ our* awareness of our breathing experience, heart-beat, and balance, to lead us into whole-body consciousness. Whole-body consciousness prepares us for the act of focusing our power of attention to our energy centers up and down the spine. These two kundalini meditation vehicles (breath awareness and chakra focusing) form the first half of our overall kundalini-awakening program. In this chapter we're going to explore the final two kundalini meditation vehicles: chanting and visual meditations.

## VOCAL MEDITATION

First let's take a beginning look at the power of spiritual vocalization, of "mantras," for generating heightened states of illumined consciousness. In his remarkable book, *The Serpent Power*, published in India at the turn of the century, Sir John Woodroffe says that "*Japa*, the Sanscrit word meaning repetition of a Mantra, can be compared to the action of a man shaking a sleeper to wake him up."

Mantras are verbalizations that we repeat over and over, which have specific effects on our nervous system due to their particular vibratory power and the overall power of the chanting experience itself. If we surrender to the experience of chanting these mantra words, we directly stimulate an awakening of kundalini power in the chakra upon which we are focusing.

Psychologically, the direct effect of chanting is to occupy the verbal part of the brain-body complex so that the usual flow of thoughts is brought to a halt. As Fritjof Capra, in *The Tao of Physics*, puts it, "The basic aim of these techniques (chanting and mandala-contemplation) is to silence the thinking mind and to shift the awareness from the rational to the intuitive mode of consciousness."

### Chanting OM

To experience a first taste of this quieting of your thinking mind, let's begin to explore the primal Yogic chant of *OM*. Let this sound flow through your mind, and perhaps awaken your vocal cords as well. *OM* actually becomes four sounds in most traditional meditative practices, as shown below. Simply let the three vowels, then the consonant, come alive in your body as your lips and tongue move to the various positions to make the sounds: *Aaaaa, Ooooh, Uuuuu, Mmmmm. . . .*

Notice that as soon as you begin to chant, even silently, your breathing begins to enter the picture as the primary force that empowers your sounds, that manifests your inner intent into actual physiological sound generation. Chanting is in fact a breath meditation.

Obviously, vocalizing is done only on the exhale; on the inhale, you are silent. Therefore, part of your chanting experience is active (on the exhale) and part is passive (on the silent inhale).

This basic pulsation from the extreme of full (inhale) to the extreme of empty (exhale) and back to full again—breath after breath for the entire duration of our lives—reflects the universal pulsation found throughout the universe. This pulsation principle is the ultimate principle of the universe. Energy, for instance, is constantly shifting into its equal and opposite, which is matter; matter, certainly at the subatomic level, is constantly shifting into its energetic form. Our breath experience is simply another primal manifestation of this pulsation principle.

When we take such a polar pulsation between opposites and stretch this pulsation out over the grid of time, we create what is called a sine wave, the basic up and down wave of all vibration, including both light and sound. To meditate on mantras and mandalas—on vocalizations and visual images—is to meditate upon the basic dynamic of the sine wave, manifest as sound and light as we personally experience it. Meditation is thus a dynamic way to focus our attention to the ultimate happenings in the universe, thus aligning our personal consciousness with the universal consciousness.

## The Chakras in Vibration

Six particular sounds are associated with the chakras in the human body. Each of these sounds creates a direct, physiological, vibrational effect on the energy centers, and also a more symbolic effect on the mind. The seventh chakra is soundless, or rather is a higher-frequency emanation of the sixth chakra's mantra, which is the mantra I taught you a moment ago, usually written *OM*. Even when you don't make a particular sound, you are constantly chanting a mantra with each breath you take, because as we saw earlier, your breathing does make a subtle sound, if you listen closely to it. In Zen Buddhist meditations, students sometimes spend years simply meditating on the sound of their own breathing. This is a very subtle approach to kundalini awakening, one that I have explored in depth and find remarkably powerful.

Pause now if you want to . . . turn your attention to your breath experience . . . and listen to the mantra of your breathing—the natural sounds created in your nose, in the subtle vibration of your bones, in your brain itself, by your inhales and exhales. Sometimes this sound is hard to hear at first, but if you listen, it will begin to arise within you. You can amplify this sound in the beginning by contracting your vocal cords and thus closing your breathing passage in the larynx just a bit. Closing your eyes also aids in focusing on the breath mantra. . . .

## The Power of Attention

At this point, I will state an obvious yet ultimate point: in all these techniques of kundalini awakening, you are putting to specific use one primary power, and that is the power of your attention. All meditation is based on the assumption that you as a human being are conscious, that you can in fact direct your attention where you want it, and that this power of attention serves to stimulate activity where it is focused.

So attention really is the key meditational tool. For kundalini awakening you can apply this power of attention in several different ways, as we are exploring with the four vehicles. But always keep in mind that your attention itself is the empowering faculty, being directed in effective ways.

## The Sound of the Universe

When you make a sound, any sound, you are in essence creating vibration where before there was no vibration. To vocalize is thus an extremely primordial act of creation.

The Tantric Buddhist tradition of Tibet speaks in its holy scriptures of the upper lip as the male sexual principle and the lower lip as the female sexual principle. In chanting, if you are aware of these opposites between which vibration is passing, you can expand your mantra experience by feeling the sound being activated by the sexual principle.

It is taught in Tibet that when you bring your two lips together in making the *Mmmmm* sound, when you unite the two sexual principles at the end of chanting *OM*, you create spiritual vibration that has magic power. In certain Tantric traditions, the *Mmmmm* is changed to *NGgggggg* for a deeper creative resonance.

When you consciously choose to create a sound, you are acting out the creation of sound. You are turning pure intent into vibrational energy. This is why chanting is so powerful. The sounds you create actually go out and set everything around you for quite some distance vibrating at the same frequencies you have broadcast. You powerfully influence the world around you with each chanted sound. If you chant the sound for the third chakra, for instance, you are sending out into the world, as a conscious act, vibrations that carry the basic energy of that third chakra.

But perhaps more important—at least for your own chakra awakening—the sound you create through vocalization also sets your own body vibrating. The sound goes out, bounces off objects in your immediate environment, and comes back to set your eardrums—and, in fact, the entire surface area of your skin—vibrating with the sound you sent out. At the same time, the sound you create directly generates internal vibrations in your air passages, your bones, in literally every cell in your body, including your brain cells.

By chanting we are making our whole being vibrate with the sound we have chosen to manifest. This is quite an act! Furthermore, not only our spiritual chants but every casual word and sound that we make throughout each day likewise directly influences us at deep vibrational levels.

I recently read an excellent article in *The New Yorker* on whales and the mystery of their songs—their long, musical, and ultimately repetitive chantings that people such as Roger Payne have been studying now for many years. "The songs [of whales] are extremely complex," Roger tells us. "They change every year, and they're very beautiful. For us they trigger many deep ideas and emotions when we listen to them. But a brutal fact is that they're monotonous. They repeat endlessly."

The article goes on to ask why whales, with such gigantic brains, seem to waste their time singing the same complex songs over and over again. The author never raises the possibility that these whales might be chanting—that instead of placing the communication of ideas as primary in their lives, they place chanting as the ultimate vocal act.

Do whales have chakras, and are they activating their chakras through their vastly beautiful and complex chantings? This is a question worth pondering. I encourage you to go out and buy a recording of whales singing, and do some of the chakra meditations you are learning while listening to the whale chants. You will find that they stimulate your energy system in unique ways.

Chanting, like breath watching and whole-body chakra watching, is a primary vehicle for shifting from symbolic mental activity to experiential awareness. To make direct contact with this shift from cognitive to intuitive consciousness through vocalization, let me encourage you to begin generating sounds that have no specific meaning to you. Humming, for instance, is the basic form of nonsymbolic sound generation.

Right now, even while reading these words, begin to hum softly to yourself, so that on your exhales, you bring into being a vibration on the theme of *Mmmmmmmmmm. . . .*

As you continue with this humming, notice where you feel the vibrational energy in your body: In your throat? In your heart? In your brain? In your solar plexus? Even way down in your sexual organs and the base of your spine?

Physiological studies have shown that every cell of your body is bathed in the sound vibrations you create in the air column of your esophagus and lung cavity. Certainly all up and down your spine your vocalization is creating an effect, even when you are softly humming.

Pause for at least a few breaths right now, close your eyes after reading this paragraph, and experience your whole body vibrating as you softly hum. . . .

## Who Needs a Master?

At this point, as we are considering vehicles that can actively help us advance spiritually, I would like to discuss further a very important matter regarding spiritual growth.

It is often said that a person must find a physical Master to give a special mantra, and in general in order for one to attempt kundalini awakening. Of course, you are blessed when a true teacher of the kundalini path comes your way. But is a formal spiritual teacher essential? The author Joseph Chilton Pearce, who has been blessed with a powerful Yogic Master with whom he spends much time each year in India, goes so far as to say that, "kundalini can only be developed when awakened and guided by the proper stimulus and nurturing, which means by a teacher who has developed his or her own kundalini under proper guidance. Unguided, or guided by a misguided teacher, the power can cause grief."

What Pearce is saying in essence is that only the lucky few who manage to find an enlightened kundalini Master can hope to evolve into higher spiritual consciousness through kundalini meditation. But in the same book, *Magical Child Matures*, he also says that the awakening of the subtle chakras is a natural development of the maturation process in all human beings, and should be encouraged in all of us. This is one of the few inconsistencies in his generally brilliant writings.

From a psychological point of view, he is encouraging all of us to consciously try to evolve into kundalini awakening. But from his own Master's warnings, he is telling us not to dare venture into kundalini meditation without a Master—even though he knows that there are very few kundalini Masters available in Western society.

My experience contradicts Pearce's. Even though I value his writings deeply in most regards, I do feel that we can approach our own spiritual advancement with the powerful tools of kundalini meditation without having to study under a spiritual teacher in the flesh.

In this regard I would like to share with you the wisdom of one of our truly inspired contemporary teachers, Bartholomew, in his book *I Come As a Brother*, a spiritual text I highly recommend reading in depth. Responding to the question, "I have heard that kundalini meditation can be very dangerous, and should be approached only under the guidance of a teacher. Is this true?" Bartholomew says, "Speaking from my own incarnative pattern, I can tell you that I did not have a guide, that I had no one around who had the slightest intimation of what I was trying to do. All I had was the movement of the energy itself. And I will tell you that it was absolutely reliable, it moved in its own way, in its own good time, it did not take me too fast, and everything was all right. . . . Do not think that you have to have a teacher for everything. The teacher is you! The power is within you, and you do have a regulatory system. . . . We live in a benificent universe, and guiding spirits are always present to help us in our explorations."

Jesus said quite simply, "Seek and it shall be found, ask and it shall be given unto you." As I mentioned earlier, the Sufi Masters of the Near East say the same thing: when you are ready for a new lesson in life, the teacher will appear, in whatever form available in your present life.

I am presently offering you guidance. I don't pretend to be an enlightened *Bodhisattva*, but I do know the basic tools of kundalini awakening. I give them to you to use in a conscious, moderate, gentle way, trusting that the Spirit will accompany my teachings and guide you through your own unique adventure of spiritual awakening, offering you teachers along the way as you need them, and offering you direct support during your meditations.

You might want to pause a moment after reading this paragraph . . . put the book aside . . . tune in to your breathing . . . your whole-body presence here in the present moment . . . feel whatever energy flows might be rushing up and down your spine right now . . . and open yourself to the presence of your own inner spiritual teacher. . . .

## VISUAL MEDITATION

Early in my psychological studies, while working at a center exploring mystic states of consciousness through the use of hypnosis, I met a fellow researcher named Jose Arguelles, who was then primarily known for his remarkable ability to draw contemporary mandalas, or spiritual paintings, for use in visual meditation. A showing of his works at the art museum at Princeton University literally swept me away for hours at a time, every afternoon I visited the gallery.

These mandalas used many traditional spiritual images drawn from such diverse cultures as the American Indians, the Tibetan Tantric Buddhists, and the Balinese silk painters. A few years later Jose and his wife Miriam published their own book called *Mandala*. In the introductory pages of the book, the authors state that "the universality of the mandala is in its one constant, the principle of the center." Mandala artwork serves the primary purpose of helping us to focus deep within our own minds through focusing on a visual rendering that aids in spiritual balancing.

In Sanskrit, the word *mandala* literally means the "centerpoint." And in fact, spiritual meditation is largely based on holding your attention on one point over a period of time, while also expanding your consciousness to include the whole that surrounds the centerpoint.

This centerpoint can be experienced both as a physical point, a symbolic center, and a time-focus where the center of time is the here and now, and we hold our attention to this centerpoint, as in breath meditation.

The paintings that Zachary Zelig has created for this book draw on all three dimensions of the centerpoint. These paintings offer a calm, clear path to finding one's visual center, and to expanding one's mind in all directions around the centerpoint.

Symbolically, Zachary has, through his deep knowledge of ancient Hindu and Tantric philosophy, created paintings of the chakras which are perfectly in harmony with the symbolic power of kundalini. Both shape and color are potent in this regard. We will explore this symbolism with each chakra we focus on in later chapters.

You will find that you can combine looking at the mandalas with the breath meditations you are learning in this book. This way, quiet contemplation of the illustration accompanying each chakra will help you expand your consciousness more and more into the infinite bliss of the present moment.

Before I discuss mandala contemplation further, I encourage you after reading this paragraph to turn to the insert of the book and simply see what experiences come to you as you look at the first-chakra drawing—and at the same time do the basic breath meditation. . . . Feel the air rushing in and out of your nose . . . listen to the sound of the air rushing through your nose . . . expand to become aware of your heartbeat . . . your balance . . . your whole body here in the present moment . . . and experience the visual impact of the illustration while you continue with the breath-awareness meditation. . . .

### The Four Ways of Seeing

Our minds can direct our eyes to take in visual stimulation in several different ways. Instinctively, the human eye looks to see whether or not something is moving—this is a survival-based programming to look first for danger, for an aggressor moving in the environment. When you look at a mandala, you will first want to let your eyes recognize the calm unmoving quality of the picture. Conscious recognition of this unmoving presence in front of you will help you to quickly relax. You will notice your breathing deepening as well.

The second way your mind and eyes work together is to perceive shape—to identify the object in front of you, so that you can run this shape through your vast memory banks and respond to the shape according to past experience. As you look at one of Zachary's mandalas, you will want to allow your eyes to look effortlessly around the edges of the shapes he has created, so that your mind receives a full, complete inner impression of the shapes. Because these shapes are archetypal structures with deep significance in the human psyche, the conscious reception of each shape is a deep spiritual input into your mind. It becomes a primary grid where your experience in meditation can reside and ultimately take off from.

The third way the eyes look is to experience the various colors coming into the brain from the outside world. This dimension of color is so important to visual meditation that we have gone to the considerable extra cost of printing Zachary's paintings in color rather than black and white. In fact, the entire universe is made up of color, since light is always vibrating at various frequencies that generate the different colors of the rainbow. As we will see in detail later on, each of the chakras is deeply associated with particular colors, and taking these colors into your mind while meditating is a powerful stimulus to the kundalini-awakening process.

The fourth dimension to the seeing process, a dimension often forgotten, is that of perceiving depth—of recognizing that there is space between you and what you are looking at. When a person is anxious, for instance, this depth perception temporarily collapses. Conversely, when we expand spiritually, depth becomes a vital, blissful dimension. When meditating on Zachary's mandalas, you will want to regularly tune in to this expanded function of seeing, which makes you aware of the air between you and what you are experiencing visually.

Allow yourself time right now to put the book aside after reading this paragraph. Tune in to your breathing, look around the room . . . find an object you enjoy looking at . . . and in proper order, look at this object first to see if it is moving or unmoving . . . second to see its shape in all its details . . . third to experience its color textures . . . fourth to experience the space between you and the object. . . .

## Seeing Everything at Once

As I pointed out in an earlier publication, *The Visual Handbook*, "We receive over 70 percent of our sensory experiences through our eyes. Most of our physical movements, our emotional responses, our mental performance, and even our deeper insights are intimately linked with the functioning of our visual system."

But for many of us, our ability to truly take in the outside world, to become vulnerable to the impact of new visions, of new vistas, becomes seriously deadened as we grow up. The spontaneous seeing capacity of a young child is almost always vastly more sensitive than is that of a person of middle age.

A deep dimension of kundalini awakening involves a new sense of seeing that comes through the meditations we will be exploring. You are probably familiar with the fact that many mystics see visions of great beauty and bliss when they are in deep meditative states. There is no way of knowing beforehand how your own inner visionary realms will awaken through kundalini meditation. But I can assure you that if you spend time regularly meditating on Zachary's mandalas, you will find that your visual dimension will begin to come alive, to surprise you—to open up vast new vistas in all your visual experiences.

Let me say one more thing about the process of seeing. The human eye-mind system can look in two basic ways—either the eyes can focus on a point in space through the convergence of the two eyes

## The "Seeing-Everything-at-Once" Meditation

Let me offer a basic visual meditation on this experience. I encourage you to do this meditation often, when you have just a moment or two in your daily routine to tune in to your breathing, and expand your visual experience.

(1) Get comfortable, preferably sitting upright so your spine and chakras are in vertical alignment with the earth's force field. . . .

(2) Close your eyes (after reading these instructions of course) and tune in to your breathing as you have learned before. . . .

(3) Become aware of your whole body at once, here in the present moment. . . .

(4) While remaining aware of your whole body, allow your eyes to open when they want to . . . and instead of focusing on a point, be aware primarily not of surface areas and objects, but of the air around you, the space between you and objects in your environment. . . .

(5) Breathe into this expanded perceptual experience, making your inner realms of consciousness most important and your visual experience secondary . . . In this expanded state of consciousness, be open to a new experience of energy flows in your body. . . .

on the same point, or they can turn just slightly apart so that the brain experiences the entire visual field as a whole, without a central-fixation point.

Don Juan Mateus, in several of the magnificent books written by Carlos Castaneda about Yaqui Indian spiritual practices, speaks of the ability to see everything at once. This is a primary spiritual way of perceiving reality—where instead of ignoring everything else around you in order to see one thing with focused attention, you expand your seeing experience, let go your fixation on a point, and experience the visual world as a perfect wholeness.

Ultimately this is what will begin to happen as you meditate on Zachary's paintings—you will find that at a certain point, your eyes let go of their first three functions mentioned earlier, and surrender to the bliss of the fourth, of coming fully into the wholeness of the present moment. Here you see everything at once in the painting, and also are aware of the air between you and the painting while you are looking. This way of seeing brings you into full participation with your environment.

# 4

# Practical Use of This Meditation Program

*In The Teachings of Buddha*, a handbook of Buddhist scriptures put out by Bukkyo Dendo Kyokai in Japan, the Buddha teaches how to approach spiritual growth and kundalini awakening. He says, "The important thing in following the path to Enlightenment is to avoid being caught and entangled in any extreme; that is, always to follow the Middle Way."

We have, of course, from ancient Greece a Socratic saying of similar import: "All things in moderation."

My general approach to kundalini awakening lies within these precepts, especially when you don't have an outside Master to guide you through your spiritual adventures.

If you are asking for extremes in your spiritual experiences, and if you ask long and hard enough, you will almost surely get them. This is what I have observed with clients who were sent to me in states of painful and frightening kundalini awakening. At one level or another, they were people who chronically pushed their limits, who craved extremes in life—and finally received extremes in spiritual dimensions as well as others.

Certain basic spiritual laws apply, which have their counterparts both in science and in everyday physical reality. These laws are based on the symmetricality of life, in which all life experience has a middle point, as we observed in mandala meditation. And this middle point has around it, in all directions, infinite extremes. If we leave the middle point in search of one extreme, we will likely at some point in our lives end up experiencing the opposite extreme as well.

This means that if we hunger after spiritual explosions of bright white light up our spinal cords, we will also be inviting times of total black depression in our nervous systems, to balance the other extreme.

The path of a wise kundalini student is to remain in the middle point, and allow that middle point to move itself up the spine through the various chakras.

Also, instead of trying to push spiritual growth faster than it would naturally evolve, it is wise to develop the discipline of holding your attention steadily at the level of spiritual energization you presently find yourself, and to gradually encourage new inflows of kundalini realization.

Another pitfall of spiritual adepts is that of hungering after Enlightenment itself, as if this were an external goal, usually placed in the seventh chakra, up in heaven beyond the physical body. I have been amazed at how often spiritual seekers I meet are compulsively chasing after Enlightenment, trying to achieve this state by pushing their meditative techniques to extremes.

Again, I find the words of the Buddha perfectly instructive in this regard, and since few people in our culture have ever read through the Buddhist scriptures, let me quote him again: "Enlightenment has no definite form or nature by which it can manifest itself; so in Enlightenment itself, there is nothing to be enlightened. Enlightenment exists solely because of delusion and ignorance; if they disappear, so will Enlightenment."

When I first heard this saying of the Buddha from Alan Watts, I was struck to the quick—because I myself was a young man hungering after Enlightenment as if it were the ultimate spiritual experience. In fact, Enlightenment is nothing more than the extreme opposite of total ignorance and delusion, as the Buddha pointed out so clearly. It is not the centerpoint at all.

So in kundalini awakening we are not seeking Enlightenment except to the extent that we are moving away from ignorance and delusion. What we are actually seeking is the middle point. This is why in our meditations we will be placing the center of kundalini awakening not up in the Crown Chakra at the top of the head, even though that is where the great spiritual fireworks are to be experienced. Instead, we are placing the centerpoint of kundalini in the heart, in the middle of the chakra system.

Once again the Buddha: "As long as people desire Enlightenment and grasp after it, it means that delusion is still with them; therefore, those who are following the way to Enlightenment must not grasp after it, and if they gain Enlightenment they must not linger in it."

## THE BREATH PENDULUM

Exactly what we have been talking about at somewhat philosophical levels can be experienced directly through breathing meditations. Your breathing is by nature a continuous swinging of an inner organic pendulum from one extreme to the other, from completely empty to completely full and then back again. To find the central point in the middle of your breath experience is one of the key centering meditations.

Most beginners of breath meditation, however, find that they habitually fixate more on one extreme than the other—they are more aware of their inhales and being full of air, for instance, than of their exhales and regular moments of being empty. Or if they have a more depressive nature, they are fixated more on their exhales.

By regularly observing your breathing in action, you begin to feel your conditioned prejudices about feeling full or empty. And as you progress along the spiritual path of kundalini awakening, you will find that through regular breath observation, the imbalances in your perception of your breathing experience begin to self-correct.

The power of attention is so remarkable that in and of itself it instigates a movement toward the middle way that the Buddha was teaching. Your challenge is simply to hold your attention on your breathing as much as possible in everything you do in daily life. The deep spiritual power of your attention will balance your mind and body.

Thaddeus Golas in *The Lazy Man's Guide to Enlightenment* appears to be completely in harmony with the Buddha. His main point is the Zen Buddhist precept that "there is nowhere to go and nothing to do" in order to attain Enlightenment. We must only realize that we are here already. The centerpoint already exists within us. We are it. Our minds must simply learn to expand their awareness so that we can see the whole picture. Instead of identifying with extremes, instead of taking sides and putting one side of reality against the other, we should consciously expand our awareness so that we see the entire scope of reality at once. This is what spiritual growth is really all about.

Kundalini awakening is a progressive realization that in fact we are energetic systems, and that the energy is flowing in both ways at once through our nervous systems—from the bottom up, and from the top down, generating the midpoint in the heart. Again we see that two extremes are involved in our spiritual experience—energy from above and energy from below.

After reading this paragraph, with your breathing coming and going as the basic bellows of your spiritual consciousness, put the book aside for a few breaths . . . be aware of yourself here in the present moment as a whole unity . . . and in this expanded state of consciousness allow your mind to reflect on this ultimate theme of balance and the middle way, in your own life. . . .

## MEDITATION LOGISTICS

At this point we need to ask ourselves specific questions about how to approach a regular kundalini meditative discipline. I myself am not a great fan of extremes when it comes to meditative discipline, because of the need for balance we have been speaking about in this chapter. So I am not going to suggest that you always get up at four in the morning and meditate. Nor am I going to suggest that you always sit for hours at a time when you meditate.

Instead, I am going to suggest that you take responsibility for finding your own definition of the middle way, in terms of your personal meditative discipline. There is no doubt that some discipline is required. But at the same time, spontaneity must be included in your meditative plan, so that those two extremes can find their own middle point.

Therefore, to the extent you feel comfortable with this, do discipline yourself to meditate at particular times of each day. But also, let your schedule be open to spontaneous meditation sessions.

Many people do like to get up perhaps half an hour early in the morning—since there seems to be special psychic energy available before the sun comes up—and meditate each day before doing anything else.

Some people prefer to meditate in the evenings, when the house is quiet again and peace can be found. There are certainly night people and morning people in this regard. Experiment and see which you prefer. And of course, it is quite excellent to meditate twice, at both morning and evening, or at midday as well.

However, we should be sure not to take these traditional times as sacrosanct. The key is this: Set aside half an hour of peaceful retreat time from your busy day, wherever you can best claim such time. Be as regular as you can, using a certain amount of discipline to motivate yourself. It does take discipline sometimes to make that beginning effort to sit up and meditate early in the morning, or to sit

· 77 ·

down and meditate at the end of the day, or sometime in between. Nurture discipline as an admirable personal quality. Without any discipline at all in spiritual realms, there will be very little spiritual growth.

In a half-hour to forty-five-minute kundalini meditation session, you will at first usually take about five minutes to do the basic breath-awareness meditations. Then you will spend between two and five minutes meditating on each chakra, employing each of the four vehicles of meditation that I will teach you for each chakra. You will work your way up through the seven chakras in turn, then finish the meditation session by devoting at least five minutes to open meditation, where you simply experience your present spiritual condition after the specific chakra meditations. This is the formal kundalini session. It should be the heart of your kundalini development.

## MEDITATION POSTURES

The traditional kundalini posture is to sit upright with the spine relatively straight. I recommend this as the normal posture. Sit calmly, but be sure to allow your body to move slightly when it wants to so that you don't feel tight and restricted. Especially when you are doing breath meditations, it is perfectly fine to allow your entire spine to move with the natural movements of the breath experience.

You can also lie on your back sometimes and experience your chakras in that position for a different experience. As Joseph Chilton Pearce comments, "My teacher told me to spend half my meditation time sitting in the conventional cross-legged style, and the other time lying flat on my back. All my meditation experiences, sensory ventures into other states, take place during this lying-down period."

It is natural that the more dreamlike dimensions of meditation are stimulated while lying down in the usual sleeping posture. My experience is the same as Pearce's—while sitting up, I go deeply into my actual present-moment spiritual exploration, whereas when I meditate lying down, I drift into those special regions of consciousness known as lucid dreams in Yaqui Indian tradition. These trancelike adventures offer a perfect balance to the intense kundalini meditations done while sitting upright. You can experiment for yourself with the proper balance between the two in your own meditation routines. Many people prefer to sit upright to begin the day in meditation, and to lie down to finish the day with more dreamlike meditation.

There is also nothing wrong with doing short chakra meditations while standing up, or while walking or running or dancing. Even while you are in action, tune in to your spine and chakras, your breathing and whole-body presence—you are a kundalini being every moment of your life. The trick is to recognize this, and take advantage of it.

Let me say a few more words about the sitting posture. If you sit on the floor in the traditional cross-legged Hindu and Buddhist position, I recommend a pillow or folded blanket under your bottom, with your knees and feet on the floor, so that your spine is raised just a bit off the floor. This position seems comfortable for most people and enables the kundalini energies to flow easily. It also relieves back pain while you hold the sitting position for long periods of time.

It is also acceptable to do kundalini meditations while sitting in a chair. However, the chair should be a straight-backed one, so that your feet are flat on the floor, your knees level with your hips, and your spine upright. Many people in our culture prefer this chair-meditation posture, at least some of the time. Experiment and see what seems best for you.

## HATHA-YOGA AND KUNDALINI AWAKENING

Several different types of Yoga have been brought over from Hindu and Buddhist traditions. They are all based on discipline, or constant practice, called *sadhana* in Sanskrit terminology. All the

Yoga techniques are designed to increase and balance kundalini energy flows in the body, and thus to make all actions in life more spiritual.

The classical musician Yehudi Menuhin has said the following about Yoga in contemporary life: "The practice of Yoga induces a primary sense of measure and proportion. Reduced to our own body, our first instrument, we learn to play it, drawing from it maximum resonance and harmony."

The techniques I am teaching in this book are often drawn from ancient teachings by such Yogic Masters as Patanjali, who, in his *Yoga Sutras*, systematized the ancient Yogic practices of his spiritual culture several thousand years ago.

These practices include hatha-yoga, which focuses on physical postures and movements for balancing and purifying the body; prana-yoga, which is the deep practice of breath control and balancing; karma-yoga, which refers to good works in the community; and kriya-yoga or kundalini-yoga, referring to the advanced mental techniques for focusing upon the chakras and energizing them.

In the *Bhagavad Gita*, another ancient spiritual text of the Hindu tradition, it is said that "when the restlessness of the mind, intellect, and self is stilled through the practice of Yoga, the Yogi by the grace of the Spirit within himself finds fulfillment." And in still another ancient text, the complex book of the *Kathopanishad*, Yoga is described in this way: "When the senses are stilled, when the mind is at rest, when the intellect wavers not—then, say the wise, is reached the highest stage. This steady control of the senses and mind has been defined as Yoga. He who attains it is free from delusion."

Instruction in any of the Yogic disciplines is of course always an enhancement of spiritual growth. For instance, if you have the chance, I strongly recommend taking a course in hatha-yoga, because working directly with the physical postures, or *asanas* as they are called, will definitely aid in your kundalini-awakening process. I myself do at least half an hour of my favorite Yoga postures each morning, because they feel good and serve me exceedingly well.

But again, it is a mistake to think that the Yogic tradition is the only path to spiritual awakening. These techniques are excellent tools for developing our spiritual presence, but at heart our spiritual awakening is something between us and the Spirit within us—not limited to particular religious doctrines or meditative techniques.

Let me give you a final description of what true Yoga is, again drawing from the *Bhagavad Gita:* "Never let the fruits of action be your motive; and never cease to work. Work in the name of the Lord, abandoning selfish desires. Be not affected by success or failure. This equipoise is called Yoga."

## How to Approach Each Chapter

As we now advance to Part II, we will be exploring one chakra at a time, a chapter for each chakra until we have explored all seven chakras in turn. In each chapter I am going to offer both additional information about the nature of each chakra, and specific meditations for you to explore to awaken each chakra. You can read quickly through the book to gain an overview of all the chakras, then return to go deeply into each chakra meditation. Or you can take your time from the beginning, spending on each chapter a day or a week to bring your inner experience into clearer focus through the meditations.

I have designed this book as a manual that you can live intimately with until you master each meditation that I am presenting. I do not expect you to assimilate everything in the first reading. The beauty of kundalini meditation is that every time you meditate upon a chakra, or upon your entire energy field as a whole, you gain a new perspective on the entire nature of your spiritual energetic system. By the time you have advanced through the meditations of all seven chakras you will find that you can reap an entirely new level of experience through returning to the chapter on the first chakra and starting over.

Let's end this chapter by exploring a simple meditation on what we've discussed thus far. See what experience comes spontaneously if you put the book aside after reading this paragraph, and make yourself comfortable in a meditation posture. . . . Let your eyes close when they want to . . . tune in to your breathing experience . . . your heartbeat or pulse . . . your sense of balance . . . experience your whole body at once, here in the eternal present moment . . .

In this state of expanded meditative calm, open yourself to whatever insights and experiences are ready to come to you from your own spiritual center, at this particular moment in your spiritual unfolding. . . .

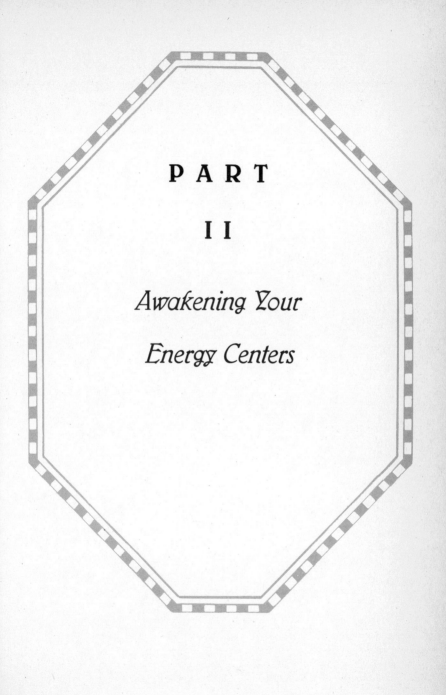

# PART

# II

*Awakening Your*

*Energy Centers*

*We're now ready to* venture into an in-depth exploration of each of the seven energy centers in your body, learning the traditional functions and general significance of each chakra, and also the specific kundalini techniques for awakening and balancing each of the energy centers in turn.

In actuality no unified world tradition regarding the nature and functioning of the seven human chakras exists. The Hindu and Buddhist traditions of India, for instance, differ significantly from the Tantric and Taoist traditions found in Tibet, China, and adjoining Buddhist regions.

Also, significant and diverse traditions regarding the human energy centers can be found in every deep spiritual tradition of all tribes and civilizations throughout the world. So-called primitive religions, for instance, abound in references to the various spirits that reside in different parts of the body. I have found some of the highest understandings of chakra functioning in some of the primitive traditions of the planet.

In Western antiquity quite a number of esoteric societies, such as the Knights Templar, the Freemasons, and the Gnostic Christian cults, dealt at very high levels with chakra systems and the use of

Christ consciousness for attaining kundalini awakening. Such authors as Ann Ree Colton in her various books, perhaps the best being *Kundalini West*, have explored these Western chakra traditions as they coincide or contradict Hindu and Buddhist models.

Although such background material is often fascinating, this book is not the proper place to spend a thousand pages in comparative chakra studies. My intention is to present a more pragmatic, experience-oriented exploration of each of the chakras, so you can use the kundalini model as a vehicle ultimately for transcending concepts and tapping directly into your own experiential energy system.

When Jesus said "know the truth, and the truth will set you free," he was almost certainly talking about knowing experiential reality directly, so that we can at least temporarily transcend our thinking, analyzing minds. There is also the beautiful statement from the Bible in which God says, "Be still, and know that I am God." This level of knowing is vastly deeper than any concept of God or Enlightenment in one's mind. As I said earlier, spiritual growth is a function of direct encounter with the divine, not an idea about such an encounter.

With this in mind, let me introduce you to a general mapping of each chakra, so that you can then fly on the wings of your own attention and take a direct look at your own chakras in action in the present moment.

# 5

# Grounding into the Earth (First Chakra)

*The first chakra, often* referred to as the Root Chakra, is most powerfully related to our contact with the Earth, our home planet. In Sanskrit the word for this chakra is *muladhara,* which translates directly as "root." And in fact, the physical nerve bundle at the base of the spine that is associated with the Root Chakra does look like a massive root system that leaves your spine and runs down both legs as the sciatic nerve. This is the largest peripheral nerve system in your body, about as thick as your thumb as it leaves the sacral plexus at the base of your pelvis and spreads like a great root system down each leg, all the way to the tips of your toes and the bottoms of your heels. This Root Chakra is considered a lowly, unimportant energy center by some people. By others, especially in recent years, it is revered with utmost respect.

When I was in my early twenties, searching for both a profession and a pathway deeper into my own spiritual life, I found myself studying with two teachers, each with opposing views on the Root Chakra. My teacher in the Yoga tradition, Kriyananda, seemed to be teaching that the Root Chakra was the lowest energy center, to be left behind as quickly and permanently as possible. Things of the Earth, of human and animal origin—of instinctive and emotional coloration—were considered lowly and even negative fixations. The great aim was to purify the body and get beyond it as quickly as possible, so that one could live up high in the celestial realms of pure light and God consciousness.

At the same time that I was studying Yoga with Kriyananda, I was also studying to become a Bioenergetic therapist under the tutelage of Alexander Lowen, the founder of the Bioenergetic tradition based on the teachings of the great psychiatrist Wilhelm Reich. I was learning from Dr. Lowen that what was most important in life was becoming more grounded to the Earth—coming down into my roots and letting go of mental delusions of spiritual and conceptual grandeur.

I found both traditions—equals yet opposites—valid and helpful in my personal life, although I sometimes felt as if the conflict between the two would drive me crazy.

I was also studying with Alan Watts at the time, a spiritual teacher for whom nothing was sacred, who knew all the traditions but preferred to live life "outside" them. He taught me one night in 1971, while we sat alone on his houseboat in Sausalito, that there was a conceptual trick that would save me from being torn apart by the two opposing philosophical and spiritual traditions of loving heaven and loving Earth.

"You must expand your consciousness so that you realize you are living within a two hundred percent universe," he said to me with a gleam in his eyes. "Just expand your mind to include both these traditions as one hundred percent true in and of themselves. Let your concept of reality expand to two hundred percent. Then both traditions can live harmoniously within you."

Of course he was simply teaching me the Chinese Taoist understanding of life, in which all dualities are encompassed by the eternal whole. I had read these notions many times before, but his words resonated deep within me, and I realized at a gut level the truth in

# THE SEVEN CHAKRAS AND RAYS

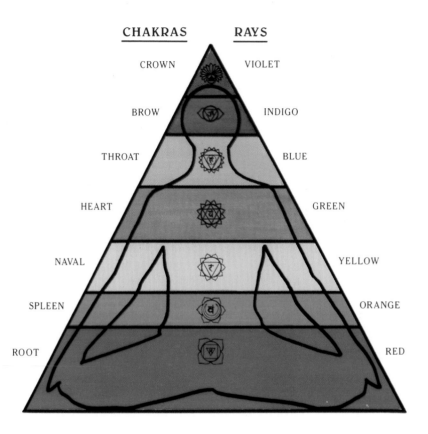

CHAKRAS          RAYS

CROWN            VIOLET

BROW             INDIGO

THROAT           BLUE

HEART            GREEN

NAVAL            YELLOW

SPLEEN           ORANGE

ROOT             RED

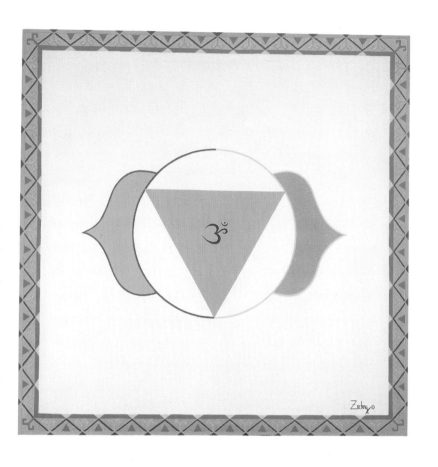

what he was saying. I have always been thankful to him for liberating me from feeling I had to choose between Hindu and Bioenergetic approaches to personal growth. After all, even while we advance upward to encounter the pure white light of the heavenly spheres, we must also bow down and give all reverence to Mother Earth.

At this point in history it is ecologically as well as spiritually important that we break free of both the Hindu and Christian attitudes that judge the lowly reality of the Earth as negative, as sinful, even as the domain of the Devil himself, and that revere only heavenly, nonearthly dimensions of consciousness. Especially from ecological points of view, "down" must be viewed as ultimately beautiful because reverence for the planet is absolutely essential if human life on this planet is to continue.

So the Root Chakra, which provides us with our connection to Mother Earth at a most primal level, should be held as equal to the Crown Chakra at the top of the head. This makes perfect sense, as we will see in practice later on, if we think of the Heart Chakra as the center of kundalini consciousness.

The chakras are in fact paired, especially in the Taoist tradition of China. Let me make this pairing of chakras clear right from the start.

The Heart Chakra, number four, is the center. If we go up and down one step, we pair the fifth chakra in the throat with the third chakra in the solar plexus/navel region. If we go up and down another step, we pair the sixth chakra, the point between the two eyebrows, with the second chakra, the Sex Chakra in the genital region. And if we make the final step, we pair the seventh chakra, the Crown Chakra, with the first chakra, the Root Chakra. Again we find this dynamism of equal extremes balancing each other.

Jesus said, again with many levels of meaning, that "the first shall be last, and the last shall be first." This certainly is a way of perceiving the Root Chakra and the Crown Chakra: they are a pair.

It is not only a spiritual violation but also an extremely dangerous practice to try to deny the bottom chakra while fixating on the top chakra.

With this roundabout but hopefully significant introduction, let me continue my discussion of the Root Chakra, the chakra that connects us to the Earth, that grounds us into our instinctive, animal, earthly needs and desires, and that ensures our survival.

Consider for a moment your own relationship with your instinctive, earthly, animal nature. Do you consider the very idea that you are an earthly animal somehow negative, or are you in love with the planet, dedicated to preserving Mother Nature, in harmony with your instinctive consciousness that guides you day in and day out? Pause and see what comes to mind, as you remain aware of your breathing and your physical presence here in the present moment. . . .

## RIDING THE PLANET

In traditional literature, the Root Chakra is said to be found equidistant between the anus and the genitals. I like to say that the first chakra is what you sit on. When you are in meditation in a sitting position and want to focus on your Root Chakra, simply turn your attention to that point where you are in touch with the Earth.

Gravity is certainly one of the determining qualities of the Root Chakra. I had a very fine teacher at one point in my life who was a Native American. He spent considerable time trying to guide me into a direct encounter with the pull of the planet I was riding through space. For him, spiritual development both began and ended with a feeling of rootedness in the Earth. No spiritual growth was possible if the Earth spirit wasn't first brought into conscious harmony with the personal spirit.

Our entire energetic nature exists within the parameters of the energetic force field of our planet. As I mentioned before, the chakras themselves, according to ancient tradition, are spinning vortexes that, if viewed from a particular distance, would look exactly like the spiraling galaxies that we see through our telescopes. Likewise atoms are miniature galaxies with their own spinning vortexes and central fixation points. So it should come as no surprise that our seven energy vortexes in our bodies are of a similar nature to the macro- and microcosms around and within us. As above, so below.

I remember vividly many direct encounters with my first chakra when I was a little boy. In the middle of spontaneous reveries, in which I would let go of thoughts and outside stimulations, I would suddenly feel myself overwhelmed by a vibrant red color that would come flooding up into me as if from the ground below me. (The color red, being the longest, slowest vibration in the color spectrum, is the color most strongly associated with the lower three chakras.)

A few moments after the flush of red came upon me, a strange spinning feeling would come right at the base of my spine, where I sat on the ground. And I would feel my body extending suddenly down, down to the center of the Earth.

I first remembered these experiences through age regression sessions I did professionally as an adult in hypnosis research. Most of us cannot remember in vivid detail such experiences that came to us in our first two or three years of life, unless we put to use age regression techniques. But I suspect that all little children have similar encounters with their first chakra, until they start to shut out such experiences as their rational minds become more active.

What do you suppose your own early-childhood experiences were of your energetic body? Quite often, people can gain vague memories of first-chakra experiences by just pausing and opening their minds to their early childhood.

Try this yourself, several times at least, in the next few days. Pause and relax a few moments . . . close your eyes . . . breathe calmly . . . turn your attention back to your early childhood . . . see if any memory traces spontaneously pop into mind, of redness, of swirling, of feeling yourself riding perfectly balanced atop your spinning planet. . . .

## GROUNDING INTO THE EARTH

We are riding this planet right now, as we have been since our conception. We live constantly within the powerful electromagnetic force field of the planet. Is it possible to be conscious of this power that defines so much of our existence, moment to moment?

I am good friends with a professor of physics at Zurich University, Eduard Cartier, who feels that much of the chakra experience of human beings is generated by the fine-tuning of a human body's electromagnetic force field with that of the Earth. I believe this is at least part of the energetic picture. It explains how we feel energy coming from above and below, for instance, since as you perhaps know, our personal electromagnetic force field looks like a magnet with curved lines of electromagnetic energy entering through the top of our head and the base of our spine, just as the Earth's electromagnetic force field enters at the North Pole and curves around to also enter at the South Pole.

Therefore, it makes perfect sense that becoming aware of the pull of gravity—and opening yourself to the actual electromagnetic power of the Earth all around you as it participates in your individual power—is an essential step to first-chakra awakening. We are immersed in this electromagnetic force field, just as a fish is immersed in water and a bird in air. Root Chakra meditation involves becoming conscious of this electromagnetic force field interacting with our own body's force field. This sounds hard to do, but in reality it is immensely easy. All it requires is learning to turn your mind's power of attention to look in a particular direction.

Let me give you time now to put the book aside after reading this paragraph. . . . Breathe . . . become aware of your whole body at once . . . feel yourself sitting on the Earth . . . become aware of the place where you meet the Earth . . . let your first chakra merge with the energetic presence of the planet . . . feel yourself energetically in alignment with the electromagnetic force field of the Earth, not just as an idea but also as an experience. . . .

## THE FOUR-PETALED LOTUS FLOWER

Each of the chakras is envisioned in classical lore as a lotus flower. Every chakra's lotus has a different number of petals. The number of petals is related both to Sanskrit symbolism concerning the configuration of subtle nerves, called *nadis*, that emanate from the particular region of the spinal column where the chakra is located, and also to the meaning of particular vowels and consonants in the Sanskrit alphabet.

The *nadis* are related to the actual physiological nerve ganglions of the body. For instance, the coccygeal-spinal ganglion at the base of the spinal cord has four primary nerve bundles emerging from it, matching the number of lotus petals for the first chakra.

I should mention here that in both Hindu and Chinese teachings, there exists, along with the physiological nerve pathways throughout the body, a more subtle system of energetic passageways in the human body. These energetic passageways channel electrical/energetic flows much like the physiological nerves channel biochemical flows of information.

Acupuncture, for instance, is based on this subtle system of energy conduits, called meridians, that exist throughout the body. Just a few decades ago, such an esoteric notion of subtle energetic passageways in the body was laughed at as preposterous by the Western medical establishment. But in a short time, modern medicine has accepted the veracity of acupuncture treatment, even though its seemingly magical results are not fully comprehended by science. We still remain in the dark ages in many respects at this point in history, whereas a much deeper understanding of energetic systems existed in ancient civilizations.

Let me share a bit more of the traditional understanding of the meaning of the four-petaled lotus flower. The most important point to keep in mind about the four-petaled lotus is that, in a relatively unawakened person, this lotus flower is envisioned as hanging downward from above the chakra. Thus the energies of this chakra are mostly being sent downward, to sustain basic survival activities of the individual.

When you meditate on this chakra for a time, sending conscious attention and energy into this region, the lotus flower begins to turn upward, so that kundalini energy flows up the spine instead of being spent only on survival activities and routine mental functionings. This is of course a symbolic image, but it carries very real relevance to what happens energetically during kundalini meditation.

I had a special teacher when I was twenty-seven, who taught me how to consciously encourage the lotus bud in each of my chakras first to open up as if to morning sunlight as the kundalini energy warmed its petals, then to raise its head upward so that there could be more of an upflow of kundalini energy through my entire nervous system. I want to pass on this image to you as well, as a vision to integrate into your chakra meditations. What is important is that you consciously encourage the lotus flower to raise its head upward, so that your energy can flow up into the higher chakras and not be spent entirely down below.

Pause if you choose to after reading this paragraph . . . put the book aside and close your eyes . . . and see if you can imagine in your mind a four-petaled red-colored flower. . . . Imagine this flower hanging down, closed as a new bud . . . now imagine the bud receiving light and warmth from your own powerful focus of attention . . . and imagine this bud opening up and raising its head, so that the new-found energy flowing through its roots can rise up and spread out from the flower, up and up into all your chakras. . . .

## SPHINCTER CONTRACTION

The next step in first-chakra awakening is exceedingly important to devote a great deal of time and patience to in meditation sessions. If you don't become deeply immersed in this special step in kundalini awakening, you can forget the rest of the program—this is crucial.

This meditation involves what you might consider one of the more lowly parts of your body. But as one of my Zen teachers once pointed out, it is to be expected that spiritual awakening must begin at the lowest point.

This technique, which I first learned from Thakin Kung and then came across in the detailed book by B. K. Iyengar, *Light on Yoga,* is a very physical way of making contact with the Root Chakra as it relates to the sphincter muscles of the anus—while using the breathing as a pump to raise kundalini energy up the spine.

The ancient Sanskrit text called the *Hatha Yoga Pradipika* says "by this technique [of sphincter-muscle contraction during Root-Chakra meditation] the yogi obtains unequalled knowledge, through the favour of the Kundalini which is roused by this process."

The technique involves sitting quietly in a cross-legged position on the floor, or on a chair if you prefer. Place your hands in your lap with one palm on top of the other so that your thumbs cross . . . let your eyes close if they choose to. . . .

Breathe slowly, encouraging energy to flow up and down your nervous system . . . and begin to let each new exhale take you deeper and deeper, down into your abdomen, and down even deeper into your pelvis with every new breath. . . .

Now on a slow exhale, gently contract your sphincter muscles, which control the gateway of your anus. At the same time, lower your chin to your chest so that the neck muscles are contracted too. Your abdomen muscles will also contract. . . . Breathe while you hold this physical contraction for one, two, or more breaths, then relax the contraction for an equal number of breaths. . . .

Continue with this meditation for as long as you like, contracting the sphincter muscles of the anus as best you can, and then relaxing for an equal period of time. . . . Be sure, from the beginning, to do the contraction in a way that feels good.

This meditation can generate remarkable effects. Again, let me suggest that it is best to walk a middle path of moderation with such a meditation. Please don't think that more is better. Do this meditation for just a few minutes at first, expanding your first-chakra meditation time slowly as the days go by. Remember—you are waking up a powerful force within you. Wake this force up gently.

This meditation serves to reverse the downward position of the lotus flower, to shut off the flow of energy going down into your legs and out of the body, so that you consciously encourage an upflow in your meditations. It is only to be done after you have meditated upon your breathing and made experiential contact with your whole body at rest in the present moment.

At first many people find it a challenge to contract the anus muscles in a meditative way. In much of Yoga, we are using muscles that have not been trained to perform very sophisticated tasks. However, you will discover that you often contract these muscles during the day anyway. Especially, you contract the anus muscles while making love. The forward thrust is accompanied by this contraction—which explains how sexual activity serves to charge the body with kundalini energy! The next time you are making love, observe how you do this first-chakra sphincter contraction meditation as a spontaneous part of the sexual experience. This observation is one of the most important ones in kundalini awakening—to see how sexuality has as its base the reversing of Root-Chakra energy so that it flows upward.

Give yourself adequate practice during every meditation session to strengthen this sphincter-contraction exercise. Do it gently, discovering the many different ways it can be done. You are developing each time you do this a special sense of mind-body harmony essential for kundalini development.

Very often during the day, remember to contract the anus muscles a few times while doing many different things. You will soon find that you enjoy this feeling of contraction. It is a direct way to encourage your sexual and survival energy to flow upward throughout the body so that your kundalini consciousness quickly becomes a regular quality in your life.

Most significantly, you will stop wasting your energy and begin increasing your basic charge in the higher chakras. Thus from the most lowly, as the Chinese proverb states, we rise to the great heights.

You will notice that you naturally also contract the abdomen muscles with this exercise, which merges the first-chakra energy with the third-chakra center, as we will see later on. Make sure that you focus on the sphincter contractions as primary. You will feel that you are doing this properly when there is an energetic tension throughout your torso from neck to anus. This tension will feel good as it aligns the spine and brings a rush of vitality throughout the chakras, as the energy surges upward from the first chakra, and downward from above to the first chakra, generating a suddenly higher level of energetic presence throughout your being. This might be experienced as white light, as electricity flowing through your system, as sudden warmth, or as some completely new feeling that you simply breathe into and allow to rush into you equally from above and below.

I am going to recommend that each time you sit down to meditate, you always begin by grounding yourself in the first chakra, even if your intent is to focus primarily on another chakra that needs balancing. In practice, it is best not to make overly firm plans regarding what to do in a meditation before you are actually

■■■■■■■■■■■■■■■■■■■■■■■■■■

## "Energy Pump" Breathing

We are now going to explore a very simple way, through your breathing, to encourage a balanced flow of energy both up into your body from below, and down into your body from above. Practice the following meditation.

(1) As you inhale, consciously focus upon the feeling of energy flowing up from the earth into your Root Chakra, and on up into your higher chakras. Inhale slowly, as if drawing this energy up gently into your chakra system.

(2) Now as you exhale slowly, open up to receive a spontaneous flow of energy from above. Experience a downflow of light, insight, and power into your body,

meditating, except to reflect upon your various meditational possibilities. Simply start at the base chakra as I am now teaching you and work your way up. Your intuitive spirit will be your guide each step of the way.

As I said before, working with one chakra is not an isolated process. Stimulating the base chakra, for instance, will also stimulate all the other chakras, since they are an energetic unity. Each time you do a sphincter contraction-relaxation meditation, pause after a certain point, relax, and feel the new energetic condition of your nervous system as a whole.

With Energy Pump breathing, you are unifying top with bottom, making conscious contact with all your chakras, with each full breath cycle. In more esoteric terms, you are unifying heaven and earth—the ultimate spiritual marriage.

moving through each of the chakras in turn until all seven chakras have been illumined from above and you are empty of air.

(3) Then again, without effort, let your next spontaneous breath come rushing into you and allow energy to flow up from the earth into your energetic system, all the way to the top chakra. (Rather than just imagining this, see if you can tune in to the actual energetic experience happening inside you.)

(4) Again, after a full inhale, reverse the experience. Begin to exhale again, opening up to the downflow of universal energy into your personal system. Continue with this pattern for a number of breaths.

Make sure you understand the entire process, reading through the descriptions until you know them by heart. Then put the book aside, practice what you have learned, and see what experience comes to you. . . .

## ROOT-CHAKRA VIBRATIONS

Now that you have learned how to tune in to your breathing, to breathe into your Root Chakra, and to bring your mind's attention to the Root Chakra through the sphincter-contraction meditation, we are in position to add the third vehicle—that of sound, of chanting— to your first-chakra meditation program.

It is said in the Sanskrit scriptures that "he who mentally and vocally utters with creative force the natural name of anything, brings into being the thing that bears that name." This belief is also found in

## First-Chakra Mantra Meditation

Let me guide you gently into the chanting magic. Here is the specific order that proves most advantageous to follow in awakening first-chakra energies:

(1) Always prepare yourself by grounding yourself through the primary breath-awareness and consciousness-expansion meditation that brings you fully into the present moment in your body (pp. 41, 50).

(2) Then do the sphincter-contraction meditation and the energy-pump breathing you just learned, to focus your mind's attention directly to the first chakra (pp. 95–99).

(3) Now be quiet a moment, let your breathing come and go effortlessly . . . and without hesitation, allow the sound for the Root Chakra to come into your mind, either *LAM* or *LANG*, depending on your preference at the moment. Let the word begin to vibrate in your mind *before* you begin any active vocalization. Simply begin to hear the sound in your inner realms of consciousness. . . .

the ancient Hebrew tradition of the Old Testament, and in most primitive tribal cultures as well. Words do have power, if invoked with intent.

When, through silent or manifest chanting, you call out the name of the Root Chakra, you are in effect bringing this chakra into existence in your consciousness—you are merging the actual energetic presence of the chakra at the base of your spine with

(4) Now, again without effort or mental pushing, allow the sound to come alive within your vocal cords, with your lips still closed. This subtle chanting is very, very powerful, and to be employed for a number of breaths before opening the lips. . . .

(5) Now, when you are ready, spontaneously let your lips open and form the *L* sound as you exhale. Make this consonant sound for perhaps half to three-fourths of your exhale, with your tongue touching the roof of your mouth . . . feel the vibration reaching down deep into your Root Chakra. . . .

(6) Now let your tongue drop away from the roof of your mouth, and allow the sound to change into the soft *A* as you continue with your long, slow, even exhale. . . .

(7) And now let either the *M* or the *NG* sound be made, spontaneously letting your system choose which sound wants to come out of you for that exhale . . . continue to hold your attention to your first chakra—this is the key action of your mind while chanting—and continue with this chanting for as long as you like. . . .

your mind's awareness of this energy center. This is powerful meditation.

The natural name of the Root Chakra, according to the ancient Yogis who learned to listen directly to the sound emanating from their awakened chakra, is *LAM* in the Hindu tradition, and a slightly altered and often more powerful *LANG* in the Tantric Buddhist tradition of Tibet and Nepal.

With *LAM*, your lips touch at the end of the chant, bringing the male and female energies, as I mentioned earlier, into union, thus activating the creative power of the word.

With *LANG*, something slightly different happens, a creative act between open lips, with a stronger resonance in the body. My teachers have generally counseled me to use the more inner, softer, feminine *LAM* when I am in a gentle mood, and *LANG* when I want a stronger energy experience for that meditation session.

My suggestion to you is the same.

Hold in mind when you chant a mantra such as *LAM* or *LANG* that you are generating vibration both within and around you, and that this vibration does not necessarily stop when you stop chanting. In fact, one of the aims of chanting is to stimulate an increased vibratory activity in your chakras for quite some time after the chanting stops.

Chanting a particular mantra is a direct way of tuning your entire nervous system to the particular vibrational qualities of each chakra. Again, you are acting through conscious intent to point your mind in directions that have traditionally proven effective for awakening kundalini energy.

Each time you chant the name of a chakra, you will make a different sound than you have ever made before. There is ultimate magic to chanting in this regard—it is always new! Your challenge is to simply let the sound come out of you—be a vehicle instead of a musical director. Let the sounds be as loud or as soft as they want to be, and surrender to the power of the vibration in your chakras.

The Hindu tradition has a remarkably sophisticated philosophy concerning sound. As we also saw in the Christian tradition, sound is considered the essence of the universe, the primordial energy from which all else manifests as matter. This idea is now being discovered as a basic law of science as well, as described by Fritjof Capra and others. And the great Sufi Master Hazrat Inayat Khan says in *The Sufi Message*, "He who knows the secret of the sounds knows the mystery of the whole universe."

The way to know the secret of the sounds is simple. Make them! Let chanting become a permanent part of your everyday routines, and you will transform your life into a kundalini symphony.

Pause now and take time to learn by heart the chanting procedure I just outlined. Do the seven-step meditation, and encounter your Root Chakra in a new way. . . .

## Root-Chakra Mandala Meditation

We are now in position to add the fourth, visual dimension to Root-Chakra meditation. I am going to explain completely the process of meditating upon Zachary's Root-Chakra mandala; then you can turn to the insert and actually do the meditation on the visual stimulus.

In Chapter 3 I taught the four ways the eyes spontaneously look at something in the environment. I want you to learn by heart this four-step process, so you can consciously go through the process with each mandala meditation you do. Very soon this will become an automatic habit of meditation.

First, look to see MOVEMENT.
Second, look to see SHAPE.
Third, look to see COLOR.
Fourth, look to see SPACE.

### Preparative Meditations

When you turn in a few moments to the insert to do the Root-Chakra visual meditation, remember that this step in the first-chakra meditation is built upon the previous steps. Before doing the visual meditation outlined above, make sure, for maximum effect, that you have prepared yourself by doing the first three steps already outlined in this chapter. Let me review briefly here, so you learn this by heart too.

*Step One*:   WHOLE-BODY EXPANSION AND
           ENERGY-PUMP BREATHING.

*Step Two*:   CHAKRA-FOCUSING MEDITATION
           (Sphincter Contraction).

*Step Three*: MANTRA-CHANTING MEDITATION
           (*LAM* or *LANG*).

*Step Four*:   MANDALA VISUAL MEDITATION
           (Root Chakra, Plate 2).

My recommendation is that each time you want to do a meditation on one particular chakra, you follow this order, employing the first and second and third meditative vehicles—then, if you have the book with you for the illustration, the fourth vehicle as well. You will want to take time to memorize the four basic meditations for each chakra so that you know them by heart. All your future success with this program is based, of course, on your devotion to actually internalizing these meditative processes.

Let me make clear the very important point that, once you have looked at the printed paintings of the visual meditations a number of times and taken them into your memory, you can also do the mandala meditations without the use of the book. You can close your eyes and visualize Zachary's paintings and activate the fourth vehicle through inner visualization. Thus you can do the full four-vehicle meditation even if you don't have the book with you.

## Encountering the Mandala

Here is the full process in short order: When you look at a chakra mandala, remember that your breath awareness is the most important focus of your attention.

(1) Close your eyes and also be aware of your whole-body presence in the present moment . . .

(2) In the exact middle of this centerpoint of your breathing, focus your attention to the physical presence of the chakra you are meditating upon . . .

(3) Let the sound for that chakra come into being inside you as you chant aloud or silently . . .

(4) Now open your eyes and look at the mandala!

What you will see as you look at the first-chakra mandala will be a downward-facing triangle in the center. The triangle is white (which symbolizes the power of the trinity). Around the triangle is a square, the square being yellow and further symbolizing the structural solidity of the first chakra. . . . A white circle surrounds the square, the circle of course symbolizing the ultimate circular unity of every dimension of the universe. . . . Then there are four lotus petals around the periphery of the circle. The lotus petals are orange and red, since the primary color of the first chakra is usually associated with these colors. . . . Then there is white space around the lotus petals, signifying the pure white light and void of human consciousness beyond thought and form. . . . Then there is a multicolored square as the encompassing visual image of the mandala. . . .

When it comes time to turn and look at the mandala, let your eyes look first to see *movement* . . . then to see all the various *shapes* that I just described . . . then to see the *colors* as primary . . . then to experience the *space* between you and the mandala, so that your own body comes into the picture as an equal reality-orient, in case you lost your breath awareness while looking at the mandala. . . .

At this point in your meditation, you and the mandala will be participating in the experience of sharing space together. The mandala is influencing your consciousness and your consciousness is influencing the mandala—you are doing an energetic dance together. . . .

### Reversing the Process

Once you have reached this point in your meditation, having activated all four vehicles for encountering the chakra you are meditating upon, continue looking at the mandala as long as you want to . . . at some point, begin to allow the *LAM* or *LANG* sound to return to your lips and body, bringing auditory vibration into harmony with the visual vibrations you are taking in through your eyes . . . then close your eyes and do the sphincter-contraction breath meditation to bring your attention even deeper into harmony with the first-chakra energy experience . . . then just relax, breathe without effort, and be open to a new experience throughout your chakra system. . . .

This is a very full meditative program. What I have just outlined will take you probably weeks, months, and perhaps even years to master. Remember, there is plenty of time. In fact, you have all the time in the world, in the universe, as you will discover as your meditations deepen. What is important, what I say to you again and again as your teacher in this regard, is that learning this process by heart is crucial to your success in tapping into your kundalini powers and pleasures, insights, and realizations.

At your leisure, turn to page 105 and practice the mandala meditation for the first chakra. Let me become silent now, so that you can explore all four vehicles of this Root-Chakra meditation. This chakra is associated by the way with the elephant, that strong, powerful, conscientious animal with a great memory and great staying power. Let the elephant-spirit come into you as you do this meditation. . . .

# 6

# Transforming Sexual Energy
# (Second Chakra)

*The key function of* the second chakra is to manifest primal creative energy in the form of functional sexual energy—which the nervous system can then transmute into higher vibrations of spiritual energy.

When I was first beginning to explore the notion of kundalini energy, I remember hearing that the Sufi Masters of the Near East believe an impotent person cannot hope to attain self-realization. This basic notion is in harmony with what we have discussed thus far regarding kundalini awakening—that one's sexual energy is an essential ingredient, an elemental pressure that provides us with the raw fuel needed for awakening the higher chakras.

In our own Christian tradition, where monks entered into celibacy as part of their spiritual discipline, it might appear that sexuality was considered to be in opposition to spiritual growth, not the driving power behind it. In fact, however, the practice of celibacy does not entail a turning off of one's sexual energies. It is rather a disciplined redirecting of that energy.

In both the Christian monastic tradition and the Tantric and Taoist kundalini techniques of meditation, ejaculation has been seen as the great enemy, for men, of spiritual realization. Sperm is considered to be the essence of masculine spiritual power, and if it is regularly thrown away and destroyed through ejaculation either during love-making or masturbation, then invaluable spiritual energy is lost.

If you are a woman reading this book, you are probably feeling right now what so many women have felt and been bothered by: the extremely masculine focus of the traditional kundalini teachings. After all, ejaculation is not a feminine process at all. Why is it that almost all the traditional treatises on sexual spirituality speak only of the male experience, as if women do not exist on the kundalini path at all, or if they do, only as sexual consorts to aid in the masculine spiritual-awakening process?

In fact, the meditative tradition has been quite chauvinistic in this regard. Luckily, at least a few modern kundalini teachers, such as Mantak Chia, are beginning to consciously work to eliminate the male bias in kundalini teachings. And I hope you find that I have been successful in eradicating from this text at least the great majority of the male-biased aspects of the traditional kundalini teachings I am passing on to you.

It is undeniably true that men and women do experience a somewhat different kundalini experience, due to their different sexual nature and physical/energetic endowments. Women by and large have an easier time with kundalini meditation because they do not have to deal with the ejaculation factor. Their sexual energies already are more internal by nature. This is one of the main reasons that many women seem to be more spontaneously intuitive and more in tune with their spiritual energies than most men.

Thus if you are a woman, you will find that learning to move your sexual energies up from your depths and into the higher chakras is usually not as difficult as it would be if you were a man, because your feminine nature is not to shoot your essence out of your body but to hold it and nurture it.

There is no question that a woman's womb and her heart are intimately connected, as a natural condition for successful motherhood. Therefore, moving one's kundalini energies up into the higher chakras, especially into the central Heart Chakra, is considered easier for a woman than for a man. I realize that I am generalizing here, but I do want to address this difference, as I have noted it in male and female clients over the years. The fact that both the Sexual and Heart Chakras are considered feminine should not be passed over lightly.

## THE EJACULATION QUESTION

If you are a man, let me say this regarding the ejaculation of your vital essence: On one hand, I do feel without doubt that the ancient Buddhists and Taoists were correct in pointing out that the energy it takes to create just one spermatozoan, one complete energetic manifestation of new life, is significant. And when you multiply this one sperm by three to five hundred million, which is the number of spermatozoa usually contained in just one ejaculation, it is obvious that a great deal of basic energy is lost with each ejaculation. Therefore, as it is said, a wise man conserves his seed, learns to hold his sexual charge longer and ejaculates less often. Perhaps at a certain point you will feel ready to learn specific techniques for holding your seed completely during intercourse. This is a fine goal, which you will be ready to delve into after perhaps six months to a year of devoted kundalini meditation. However, total sperm withholding is by no means necessary for successful kundalini meditation.

My general advice at this point in your kundalini development, and the path of this book throughout, is that of moderation, as the Buddha recommended. I am suggesting that you come to consciously value your sexual essence and spend it with full cognizance of what you are in fact doing each time you ejaculate. This expansion of consciousness in sexual realms will, in and of itself, begin to alter your ejaculation patterns in the direction of moderation.

It should be mentioned at least briefly that ejaculation is not the same as orgasm. Men of high spiritual development hold their sperm while experiencing remarkable, seven-chakra orgasms. In this way, men come to experience their sexuality in more "feminine" ways. They have a multitude of orgasms, of kundalini energy rushing throughout their seven chakras, without necessarily ejaculating. In this regard a man learns a vast amount about kundalini bliss through tuning in to his own feminine nature in the three feminine chakras, and through learning from intimate female friends as well. I have spoken of this in depth in *Peak Sexual Experience*.

Whether you are a woman or a man, you will quickly find, after practicing kundalini meditation in solitude, that your sexual experiences with your partner become beautifully transformed as you open yourself more and more to the flow of sexual energy into the higher chakras while making love.

Spiritually awake sexual couples for countless generations have known directly of the presence of kundalini energy and have used it according to their own natural spiritual level of awareness. And since time immemorial, the second chakra has been known and employed as a vehicle for spiritual awakening. Extremely old Egyptian, Sumerian, Mayan, Incan, and Burmese writings—to list just a few of the archaeological finds—portray the second chakra as a primal spiritual center.

## THE SEXUAL CHAKRA IN ACTION

There is not a definite line one can draw between our first-chakra and second-chakra realms of experience. The physical sexual organs seem to reside both in the first and the second energy centers. In the first, earthly chakra, the sexual organs are linked with our reproductive instincts, with propagating and raising the new generation of our species. In the second, sexual chakra, whose primary element by the way is not earth but water, our sexual organs are associated with the actual flow of seminal and vaginal fluids, with the act of making love—with tapping into the creative kundalini energy that lies coiled in the first chakra waiting to be awoken.

We all know the feeling of the kundalini energy waking up deep down inside us when we are becoming sexually excited. It is a most definite physiological sensation as the sexual energy rushes up into our genitals. We usually feel this rush not only in the genital region, but as a hot electric flush of energy up and down our spines and throughout our entire nervous system.

This experience of a wild ecstatic surge of sexual energy as we become sexually charged offers us a basic common orientation for talking about kundalini energy. The sexual experience defines a major element of the kundalini spirit manifesting in the present moment. What we then do with this energy determines how the kundalini energy affects our various chakras.

In Hindu scriptures, the second chakra is to be found not only in the genitals themselves, but up toward the navel. This is in fact the point in the spine where the sexual ganglia leave the spinal cord and move down and forward to the sexual organs. You can begin to notice for yourself with more and more clarity, when you become sexually excited, how your attention moves directly to your sexual center— and you will discover for yourself where your own second chakra is located in your body.

Let me pause and give you time to turn your attention in the directions we have just been talking about . . . first to your breathing experience here in the present moment . . . then to your whole body as an energetic system . . . and then to your Sexual Chakra. . . . Close your eyes after reading this paragraph . . . let yourself drift a bit into your past, to remember a recent experience when you became sexually aroused . . . relive the energetic experience of your second chakra coming awake. . . .

## SEXUAL YIN AND YANG

Perhaps you have heard of the Chinese Taoist way of viewing everything in the universe in terms of the opposite polarities called *yin* and *yang*, related to the feminine and masculine qualities of the universe. These spiritual terms are exactly equivalent to the nonjudgmental scientific terms "negative" and "positive" when referring to electrical charges of energy in atomic and subatomic structures.

I find this model extremely important when exploring the nature of our energetic centers in the body. The first chakra, for instance, being of the Earth, is solid, relatively unyielding, and is considered masculine yang in quality. The second chakra, which is intimately related to the element of water—with seminal and vaginal liquids which are by nature always flowing—is considered feminine yin in quality. As we rise up from the first to the second chakra, the kundalini energy is transformed from masculine to feminine. A polarity is created in our energetic system—and from this polarity springs forth creative power, just as it does in subatomic physics.

We saw that the first chakra provides the basic energy for strong masculine actions related to survival. Now the second chakra shifts to the opposite of this external type of power and brings us the nurturing, emotional, feminine power needed to conceive and give birth to a new delicate being.

An essential point to understand in relating with your chakras is that this interplay between opposites reflects the dynamic nature of your entire energetic system. From polar opposites comes manifestation—this is the teaching both of the ancient Masters and contemporary scientific masters as well. Our sexual nature dramatically expresses this reality.

## Polarity in the Chakra System

Let me briefly lay out the overall picture of yin and yang, of feminine and masculine, of yielding and unyielding, as this polarity manifests in the seven chakras:

The first chakra (Earth) is masculine; solid; earthly; yang.

The second chakra (Sex) is feminine; liquid; flowing; yin.

The third chakra (Power) is masculine again; willful; yang.

The fourth chakra (Heart) is feminine; loving; integrating; yin.

The fifth chakra (Throat) is masculine; manifesting; logical; yang.

The sixth chakra (Brow) is feminine; intuitive; mysterious; yin.

The seventh chakra (Crown) is masculine; pure bright light; yang.

Because the Heart Chakra, being feminine, lies at the crucial midpoint of the seven chakras, the imbalance between the four yang chakras and the three yin chakras is compensated perfectly. However, this is only true when the Heart Chakra is made most important as the centering, balancing chakra for the entire energy system. In some of the Hindu schools of Yoga where the Crown Chakra is the primary chakra, there is generated, instead of a male-female balance in the heart, a very masculine blasting of energy up and out the top of the head. I do not teach this type of meditation, but it does exist—to satisfy personalities that are hungering for the "great bang" experience.

I recommend that you reflect on the chart above and memorize this primary yin-yang way of viewing the chakras. Please keep in mind that the concepts of yin and yang, of masculine and feminine, are concepts you will continue to develop into new realms of understanding, as your experiential knowledge of the chakras expands beyond culturally conditioned notions.

I have found that the Taoist tradition of ancient China seems to express the deepest understanding of the inherent unity and harmony of the two polar opposites. Both yin and yang are considered equally important in all ways. Our tradition, on the other hand, is extremely biased in favor of the yang—the hard, the masculine, the tough and aggressive polarity. One of the beautiful effects of kundalini meditation, when approached as we are learning in this book, is to help us to regain a perfect balance between masculine and feminine, between above and below, between strong and yielding—between yang and yin.

## THE CONSTANT OF CHANGE

Another dynamic, which is important to keep in mind while doing kundalini meditations, is the fact that everything in the universe is constantly changing from yin to yang and then back again. In Chinese scriptures we read over and over the basic principle—that the only unchangeable truth in life is that everything is constantly in the process of changing. Night becomes day, light turns into darkness, and then inevitably, the light returns in due time, and the cycles of life continue to repeat themselves endlessly, but always in new ways.

The basic movement in lovemaking reflects this, with the proverbial "in-out-in-out" dynamic, the forward-back-forward-back movement of the pelvis. We charge ourselves with kundalini energy through this movement. In like manner, as we have already seen, our breathing constantly shifts from inhale to exhale and back again. Perhaps you now understand a bit better why the simple act of watching your breathing generates such remarkable balancing as well as charging effects in your energetic system. With each new breath cycle, you tap into the basic truth of the universe—that even though we might repeat the same basic process over and over again, still nothing remains the same, each thrust and each breath is new. Change, therefore, is the ultimate reality upon which to base our lives.

Because each chakra is surrounded by chakras of an opposite charge, there is a constant interaction between the chakras as the dance between yin and yang continues. When we become overly fixated in one of the chakras, we disturb the essential balance of yin and yang in our bodies, and end up either physically sick, emotionally disturbed, mentally confused, or spiritually unbalanced—or all of the above together.

This is why I recommend in each kundalini session that you tune in to each of the chakras in turn, so that the balancing process can take place on a regular basis. Your conscious attention focused to each of the chakras one after the other is the missing ingredient needed for such energetic balancing.

Dr. Rene Dubos, in the watershed medical book *Man, Medicine and Environment*, concisely describes the natural tendency of the human organism to seek this balance, or "homeostasis" as it is called in medical terms. The body knows how to regain balance if we focus our meditative attention to the centers that need balancing. I developed this point into a full healing program in my book *Conscious Healing*, where the principles of chakra balancing are applied to physical recovery from illness and injury. Hopefully, however, as you master kundalini meditation, you will not have to fall physically ill before learning how to regain inner balance in your energetic system.

## EMOTIONS AND THE SECOND CHAKRA

It is said as a quick generalization in many chakra books that all our desires and emotional hungers emanate from our second chakra. But upon closer observation, the first chakra, as we have seen, deals with our survival instincts and related emotions. Fear, for instance, is considered a first-chakra emotion. So are greed and possessiveness. In fact, we speak of people as being "tight-assed" if they are afraid to lose their physical possessions that ensure their security. The "fight or flight" reaction in the face of danger is also a first-chakra emotional response.

Now, with the second chakra, we move into the more subtle, interpersonal emotions. The Sanskrit word for the second chakra is appropriately *svadhisthana*, which comes from the linguistic root meaning "to sweeten." Our presexual and sexual desires for intimacy with another person certainly do sweeten our lives very beautifully, adding emotions that transcend our survival-based first-chakra emotions.

In harmony with the primal element of water, which is considered to be the key element of the Sexual Chakra, our emotions often feel as if they come flowing out of us like great liquid gushings. The word "emotion" comes from the Latin *movere*, which means "to move" and *e*, which means "out." The second chakra is deeply linked to our emotional movements and to movement in all regards.

Emotions are often experienced as existing under the calm surface of our lives, rising up unexpectedly to break into the present moment like a waterdragon surfacing in a primordial lagoon. In fact, the animal symbol for the second chakra is a waterdragon. In the Hindu tradition, this mysterious creature, like the Loch Ness Monster, lives just under the surface of our mind's ability to perceive it and manipulate it. In a similar manner, our sexual energies and emotions lie just below the surface of our consciousness, only to suddenly rise up with sometimes fearful power when we shift into sexual modes of consciousness.

To open up to the energy of the first chakra rising into the second chakra is always a surrender, a letting go of the masculine control of the first chakra, and an opening to deeper human emotions that defy control. The waterdragon is not able to live in captivity, as many old Asian and European myths say—it would rather die than lose its freedom of liquid movement.

When you are meditating it is very important to remember, as you shift your attention from the first chakra to the second, to open yourself to a liquid, feminine, emotional surrender to the power of this chakra. In traditional Hindu folklore, the kundalini energy is always portrayed as a feminine goddess, and to awaken this latent power of the kundalini is definitely to awaken a feminine power.

If you find that you are afraid of the mysterious, feminine, yin dimensions of your energy system, then you will want to devote considerable time and focus to the breathing meditations you have

already learned, especially going deeper and deeper into your exhales, being empty for longer periods of time, getting to know the
depths of your being—and learning to love this empty quality, this
feeling of feminine surrender. Otherwise your entire spiritual development will be hindered. A great deal of this book is aimed at gently
encouraging this surrender.

## KUNDALINI-RISING BREATH MEDITATION

Now that we have considered these theoretical reflections on the
nature of the second chakra, it is time to introduce the first technique
for directly contacting and activating this energy center. Your
breathing—the first vehicle—is where we begin.

You remember the energy-pump breath meditation I taught you
already in which with every inhale you allow increased energy to flow
up into your body, and with every exhale you allow increased energy
to flow down into your body. The second-chakra breathing technique
begins with this balanced-breathing pattern, then shifts it into a
specific process that brings energy from the first chakra up into the
second chakra as a conscious act of will.

What we are doing with this kundalini-rising breath meditation
is critical to all the later steps in this program. We are awakening the
kundalini waterdragon so that its vast feminine power can surge
upward and break the surface of our consciousness. We are using our
willpower to turn the lotus flower upward, so that the magical sexual
energy lying dormant at the base of the spine can rise.

Very often the energy that comes into your second chakra is not
a dramatic sexual charge at all. I have said already that this energy is
subtle. The sexual center, although I speak of it as in the physical
genitals, is actually an energetic vortex that should not be identified
too closely with the physical sexual organs. The more you do this
charging exercise, the more you will come to know for yourself exactly
what the nature of this energy is. Experience is key.

Spend some time right now exploring what sensations come to you when you begin to do this kundalini-rising breath meditation. If at first you don't feel much of anything, this is perfectly all right. You are learning a very sophisticated technique, even though it might appear simple. You are using consciousness itself to generate a flow of the lifeforce into your Sexual Chakra. See what comes to you now as you follow the instructions and open yourself to second-chakra activation. . . .

## SITTING ATOP YOUR KUNDALINI CHARGE

Many Hindu teachings encourage the meditator to visualize a beautiful young naked woman eager for sexual intercourse (again note the male bias), and to use this sexually exciting fantasy image to awaken second-chakra sexual upflows. I am not categorically against this as an occasional adjunct to this phase of kundalini awakening. But be very careful not to get too caught up in sexual fantasies at this point. In this regard I find such popular kundalini books as *Sexual Secrets* to be seriously misleading and superficial in encouraging a somewhat pornographic approach to kundalini stimulation. Kundalini meditation is not masturbation, and you want to be careful you don't activate your old masturbatory habits when doing this extremely important meditation.

With that word of caution, I want to give you some guidance in terms of sometimes using sexual fantasy to awaken kundalini energy. If you want to experiment with the traditional Hindu fantasies, I recommend the following general pattern:

> If you are a woman, imagine that you are sitting naked in the lap of a powerful man, and that his erect penis is inside you. He is holding perfectly still inside you, and you can feel his masculine power interacting with your feminine sexual power. . . .

## The Kundalini-Rising Breath Meditation

(1) As you inhale, imagine that you are drawing up energy of a sexual nature from the depths of your first chakra, so that it flows into your genitals. . . . Hold your breath a moment on full, letting the charge of sexual power be absorbed by your second chakra. . . .

(2) Then simply let the air fall out of your lungs as you exhale. . . . Don't place any attention on the exhale at all, just become empty in an effortless way, like a bucket that is being dropped down a well shaft to where the water is, deep down below. . . .

(3) Now consciously begin to pull the water up with your bucket of attention. . . . Let yourself feel a subtle rush of pleasure as you feel the sexual energy rising up higher and higher toward the surface of your second-chakra awareness. (You will want to have your spine

If you are a man, imagine that you are sitting cross-legged with a beautiful woman in your lap, with your erect penis inside her. You are breathing calmly, not moving, just tuning in to the powerful energetic happening in your second chakra as your energy center interacts with the woman's sexual center. . . .

This is the basic approach to using sexual fantasy to stimulate your kundalini charge. Use this technique if you like, or variations on the general theme, but also devote a goodly amount of meditation time to nonfantasy experiences.

You will find after perhaps a week of nonfantasy meditation on

straight as you do this if you are sitting while meditating.)

(4) Now pause again at the top of your inhale, and feel
this new bucket of primordial sexual energy charging
your genitals with yet a higher charge of sexual power
and pleasure. (You can also let this energy go rushing
higher up your spine, effortlessly, into the other
chakras, all the way to the top of your head. But if
you are someone who has a bit of a fear of a high
sexual charge in your genitals, be sure that you continue focusing on the second chakra as primary with
this kundalini-rising breath meditation.)

(5) Now again exhale down deeply and effortlessly to
your depths, and continue with this upward movement of sexual energy until you feel you have a goodly
charge in your genitals.

the second chakra that a natural, gentle, and very beautiful surge of
blissful sensations will rise up with each new breath. The key at this
point is this—only charge yourself with the amount of sexual energy
you can sit on without having to release through masturbation. Most
beginners in this technique slip too easily into too high a charge in
their genitals, and then are unable to remain calm enough to continue
with the kundalini process of transforming this energy and sending it
up to activate the higher chakras.

I am not being judgmental, nor should you feel any remorse,
if you sometimes succumb to masturbation as you are learning
this technique of second-chakra charging. Simply observe yourself
in action, and step-by-step discover how many breaths of sexual

charging you can receive from your depths and still remain meditatively calm.

## SECOND-CHAKRA FOCUSING MEDITATION

We now come to the activation of the Sexual Chakra through the second vehicle of kundalini meditation—that of learning more and more deeply how to focus your mind's power of attention to the actual location of this energy vortex in your body. Let me guide you through the basic process you will want to learn by heart.

First, it is essential always to go first through the Root-Chakra awakening process, which focuses upon the primal experience of contracting the sphincter muscle. This is the foundation for second-chakra awakening.

Let me speak a bit more about this sphincter muscle issue, since it is almost always somewhat of a stumbling block in the beginning for kundalini students. No one quite knows why shifting the mind's attention to this muscle is so powerful. But what is experienced is a definite closing of the downward flow of one's lifeforce energy, and a reversal of this flow upward. In a very real sense, as you will experience more and more pleasurably each time you make this conscious act of contracting the sphincter muscle, you are closing an energetic valve when you use your mind's attention to consciously tighten the sphincter muscle. You are using your power of will at a crucial point in your energetic body to turn the tide and shift your lifeforce flow upward. In essence, this tension in the sphincter muscle is the platform upon which kundalini consciousness is built.

Once the sphincter muscle is awakened, you can shift your mind's power of attention up one notch to the genitals. But you will find that all during the ensuing higher-chakra focusing, you naturally tend to hold the sphincter muscle somewhat contracted, once you have practiced first-chakra meditation for several weeks on a regular basis.

(Each time you do this breath-awareness meditation that leads you beyond thoughts and into the eternal present, you will find that you get better and quicker at the meditation, so that it happens not as a series of isolated expansions but almost at once as soon as you think of doing it. This is the beautiful power of routine and habit in meditation—that you can move quickly through realms of consciousness you have already mastered.)

Go ahead and explore this process in depth now. If you find that you have overcharged yourself, breathe through the mouth for a few breaths and concentrate on your exhales so that you consciously send some of your sexual charge back down from where it came.

## THE SECOND-CHAKRA MANTRA

The sound of the second chakra is actually very similar to the first-chakra sound of *LAM* or *LANG*, but at the same time it is radically different in its effect on your consciousness and nervous system.

The first three or four times I did these chants, by the way, I confess I didn't really feel much of anything. Only because my teacher encouraged me to continue, regardless of the effects on my consciousness at the beginning, did I persevere—and I now pass on this lesson to you.

It takes a certain amount of time, a week or so of devoted chanting, for the nervous system to tune itself to these sounds. It is the same with any new type of sound or music you hear. At first it sounds strange and somehow meaningless. Then, as you learn to listen and participate more deeply, vast vistas of subtlety and meaning, of pleasure and impact, are experienced.

I remember, for instance, flying for the first time up to visit a small village in the Drakensberg Mountains of southern Africa, where the Basutu tribe lives. When I landed and got off the mail plane, the sounds of the tribespeople talking all around me were like gibberish. I felt surrounded by a totally meaningless array of sounds.

▪▪▪▪▪▪▪▪▪▪▪▪▪▪▪▪▪▪▪▪▪▪

## Second-Chakra Focusing Meditation

(1) First, go through the basic procedure of becoming more aware of the air flowing in and out through your nose . . . expand your awareness to include the sounds made by your breathing . . . now expand your awareness to include the movements in your chest and belly as you breathe . . . expand again to include your heartbeat and your whole body here in the present moment. . . .

(2) Now expand your awareness to focus on your first chakra . . . constrict your sphincter muscle to close the doorway at the bottom of your energetic system, and periodically throughout this meditation constrict the sphincter muscle again . . . let the chant *LAM* or *LANG* rise up and manifest inside you, perhaps vocally as well, to awaken the Root Chakra in your consciousness . . . now visualize or look at the Root-Chakra mandala to awaken the visual dimension of the meditation. . . .

But after a short while these same sounds began to take shape, to convey meaning, to please my ears and wake up my mind. It will be the same with these simple sounds I am teaching you, when you begin to let them resonate deep within your psyche.

These mantras are what one calls essence-sounds. They have been heard deep in meditation both by the great Masters of ancient times and by contemporary Masters as well, as emanating directly from the chakra centers. As I mentioned earlier, the chakras are swirling vortexes of energy, and this swirling creates a particular

(3) Next, expand your focus of attention by doing the kundalini-rising breath meditation you just learned, charging your sexual center, with every new inhale, with more and more vibrant sexual energy. . . .

(4) Now allow your attention to move fully up into the genital region of your body . . . be open to a liquid melting sensation in your genitals as you focus upon them . . . with every new exhale, empty yourself of thoughts as you plunge down into the depths of your pelvis . . . and with every new inhale, bring up into your genitals more sexual energy . . . allow your pelvis to move slightly as you breathe. . . .

(5) Now (before you overcharge yourself) breathe in a calm, balanced manner, as you remain centered in the midst of the heightened energetic condition in your second chakra. . . .

tone, just as a swirling top will make a whistling sound. The chakras, though, have an infinitely more complex vibrational quality.

The sound of each chakra is in fact a vast symphony. And each person's chakras make a symphonic sound unique to that person. So we are on the edge of a remarkably vast realm of reality when we begin to tune in to the subtle vibratory harmonics being generated by the energy centers in both our own bodies and those of people around us.

Let these sounds come gently to you. Simply turn your attention in their direction, and open yourself to the flow of sound emerging from your own chakra depths, as you awaken this outpouring through your own chanting.

The sound of the Sexual Chakra is *VAM* or *VANG*. Let the *Vvvvvvvvvvvvvvvvvvvvvvvvvvv* sound linger between your lips for at least half of your exhale, then move into the *am* or *ang* ending. . . . Feel the vibration deep in your genitals. . . .

## The Six-Petal Mandala

Let me now introduce you to the six-petal second-chakra mandala created by Zachary. Before you turn to meditate on this sexual mandala, I will describe briefly what you will find.

The six petals of the second-chakra lotus reflect the various intensities of the emotions of the second chakra, from cool blue to hot red and everything in between. These six lotus petals are also an expression of the six *nadis* that exit the spine at this region.

Also included in Zachary's painting of the second chakra is a crescent moon, the moon being the dominant planetary force in the second chakra—a yin, feminine presence.

As explained before, I recommend that you first look at such a mandala for movement, or lack of it, to establish it in space as nonmoving and therefore nonthreatening. . . .

Then look to see the shapes in the mandala. From the center emerge the six petals, spreading your perception in all directions. . . .

Then look to see color, all the various colors of the rainbow in one circular vision, representing all your emotional colorations, all your sexual passions. . . .

Then look to see the mandala in space, and the air between you and the illustration, so that your own presence becomes as real as the illustration you are looking at. . . .

Now relax . . . see the whole visual image at once . . . and let the sound *VAM* or *VANG* again resonate throughout your being. . . .

Now bring your entire awareness again to the location of your second chakra . . . breathe into whatever experience comes to you as you allow powerful sexual energy to flood beautifully throughout your entire chakra system. . . .

Take time now to explore this full first- and second-chakra meditation you have learned thus far. . . .

# 7

# Fire in Your Navel
# (Third Chakra)

*The third chakra is* a beautifully complex energy center; it deals with personal power, organizational capacity, and the ability to go into action to manifest our ideas in the physical world. This chakra is also linked with the tendency to employ occult powers to manipulate the environment and fellow human beings. In a more positive light, third-chakra willpower is used to initiate contact with the spiritual dimensions of life that become more fully developed as we awaken the higher chakras.

Some of us are overly fixated on this willpower chakra, acting as manipulators instead of participants in life's intimate, social, and business realms. Others are weak in this chakra, afraid of our own inherent power, and therefore unable to manifest our dreams successfully. This chapter is dedicated to a bright third alternative—to using willpower for transforming kundalini energy into its next higher manifestation, which is love.

I want to share with you a number of different themes that define the third chakra so that you come to a deeper conceptual understanding of the will center. We will then devote the final half of the chapter to the actual four vehicles of kundalini meditation that generate experiential awakening of this chakra.

## PRIMAL ELEMENTS

You will remember that the first two chakras were associated with a particular element. The Root Chakra is embedded in earth, and the Sex Chakra in water. As we move up the chakra system, we discover the third energy center, the Power Chakra, aflame with the element of fire. If we look one step higher to the fourth chakra, in the heart, we find this chakra imbued with the mystic quality of air or, as it is called in ancient Sanskrit, *prana*.

Thus in the human torso, in the spinal column below the neck, are to be found all four basic elements of earth, water, fire, and air, interacting intimately with each other, yet quite distinct from each other as well.

Once we rise up into the fifth chakra, in the throat, we discover yet another basic element, that of sound—of vibration manifesting as auditory energy. This element, although sometimes not included in the basic list, certainly lies at the center in most spiritual traditions. In the Christian tradition there is the basic belief, "In the beginning was the Word [primal sound vibration] and the Word was with God, and the Word was God." The Hindu tradition considers sound equally important—as the ultimate vibratory energy of the created universe.

When we move up into the sixth chakra, between the eyebrows, we find an energy center that both receives and manifests light as its primal element. Again, in our Western religious heritage, Jesus is quoted as saying "I am the Light." In modern science, the speed of light is considered by physicists as an ultimate parameter of the known universe.

Finally, as we move up into the Crown Chakra, we discover a spiritual quality that is really beyond words, beyond labels, even though some adepts affix terms such as "thought" or "Christ consciousness" or "supreme knowledge" to this chakra. This is a level of reality that is beyond the ability of the human mind to comprehend, and yet we can experience it directly, enter into its infinite presence—

even if, when we return, we cannot quite define what we have experienced.

Because each of these basic elements is in fact of a different level of vibratory energy, it makes sense that they are located in different regions of the human nervous system, and also that as the vibrations become more subtle, they are found higher up the nervous system.

## THE ELEMENT OF FIRE

This morning, as usual for the last few months, my two-year-old son and I went outside before the sun was up. He has the spontaneous habit that spiritual adepts struggle to attain—that of waking up at the first touch of dawn. I find it somehow significant that most young children naturally get up at this vibrant time of the early morning.

We sat on the front porch and listened to the birds in the nearby trees. We watched as the occasional white cloud billowed overhead, and waited for the sun to begin to turn the clouds blushing pink, then fire red. Then finally the sun itself winked through the leaves at us, flashed its first rays into our eyes, and touched us directly.

My son never tires of this morning ritual, never fails to become excited as the sun rises up into his life for a new day. I myself, after thousands of sunrises, am still moved by each new sunrise. I'm sure you feel the same if you observe the sunrise in your daily life.

I am just biding my time until I can teach my son the poem by William Wordsworth that was the epiphany of my early-childhood poetic world:

> *My heart leaps up when I behold*
> *A rainbow in the sky:*
> *So was it when my life began;*
> *So is it now I am a man;*
> *So be it when I shall grow old.*
> *Or let me die!*

To be in awe of the presence of the sun in our lives is simply to be responsive as human beings. Our basic grounding as human beings is in the Earth. Our parallel element, from the womb thereafter, is of a liquid, watery nature. But without the sun, without fire, without combustion, there would be no life at all in this earthly, watery existence of ours. The sun is the explosion that brings new life into being. And the third chakra is the energy center that brings the power of the sun into our lives, that moves us beyond the polarity, the duality, of the first two chakras, and into a radically different, triangular type of energetic system.

## LOCATING THE POWER CHAKRA

The third chakra is often assigned to the region we call the solar plexus. By this name, the medical tradition recognizes the presence of sun energy in this region of the body. However, the third chakra also covers a region that extends down from the solar plexus to below the navel. In many Hindu scriptures the third chakra is in fact called the Navel Chakra.

In China and other Eastern countries, where the third chakra has received much attention over the centuries in martial arts traditions, this region is usually located a bit below the belly button. It is called the Chi center, whence emanates the proverbial Chi energy that is the powerhouse of all martial arts disciplines. In like manner, the Native Americans of the Zuni, Yaqui, and Huichole tribes locate the power center just down from and a bit on the left side of the belly button.

We should always keep in mind when trying to locate the chakras that they are not static, fixed entities. They are located in slightly different places in different bodies, for instance. And they also drift a bit up and down the spine depending on one's emotional and spiritual condition.

## Power-Chakra Awakening

I recommend the following simple exercise be put to use when you want to make experiential contact with your own power center.

(1) After reading this paragraph, put the book aside a moment and stand up. A good stretch is always worthwhile, so let yourself indulge in a stretch and a few yawns to bring your whole body awake. . . .

(2) Now stand with your feet fairly wide apart and toes pointed straight forward . . . bend your knees a bit . . . and with palms up, make fists with both hands. . . .

(3) Exhale with a strong *Ha!* sound as you contract your belly muscles, and also your hand and arm muscles. . . . Now as you inhale, relax your belly and hands and let your pelvis rotate back a little. . . . Now as you exhale again, contract your muscles and feel your power deep down in your belly. . . . Relax as you inhale . . . contract as you exhale . . . and continue several more breath cycles with this third-chakra activation exercise. . . . Feel power rushing up through your system as you turn your attention strongly to your Chi energy deep down in your belly. . . .

## THIRD-CHAKRA CIVILIZATIONS

Many times in my studies, I have come across teachers spreading the idea that as a world civilization, we are presently caught up in resolving destructive third-chakra imbalances, so that we can finally move forward into a fourth-chakra, heart-centered period of human civilization. In *Wheels of Life*, Anodea Judith states that "in terms of evolution, our culture is presently working its way through the latter part of the third chakra." Joseph Chilton Pearce and Gopi Krishna arrive at similar conclusions in their writings.

The third chakra is definitely associated with the ability of human beings to manipulate their environment, to willfully lay out plans and act to bring them to fruition. Technology is the great contemporary expression of third-chakra action, in that technology is a means of gaining control over the various energy sources on our planet—such as wind, sun, gravity, combustion, and nuclear fusion.

From our two bottom chakras emerge powerful desires, which provoke us into action, into movement to seek out satisfaction of our desires. The practical purpose of the third chakra, that of will, is to bring a sense of logic, planning, and gratification to our needs and urges.

Traditionally the third chakra is associated with the logical functions of the mind that enable us to make plans to manipulate the environment to our advantage. It is here that mind meets emotion, that the potential of the thinking mind is first awakened and put to use for basic plans and actions. The development of technology is a final outcome of this willful activity of the third chakra.

Beyond the basic third-chakra impetus to bring about change through technological manipulations, there is also the more ancient practice of using third-chakra power for occult manipulations. Tribal witch doctor traditions show the tendency of human beings to use willpower for manipulating the more subtle dimensions of human community. Throughout history there are records of ongoing occult practices.

Recent history also carries definite expressions of third-chakra power being used in dubious ways to manipulate other people. I think it would be fair, for instance, to say that such people as Rasputin, the powerful monk of Russian history, and certainly Hitler in modern

European history, were hyperactive in the third chakra, without adequate fourth-chakra awakening to turn their powers in compassionate directions. The American business atmosphere of the eighties certainly displayed this imbalanced third-chakra power-play condition as well. And most of the dictators of the last fifty years who have heartlessly damaged or destroyed the lives of countless millions of people have displayed in gross form a hyperactive third chakra blocked to fourth-chakra energy downflows.

This energy center is raw power, which can manifest as violence, hatred, manipulation, and cold-hearted aggression, or as a completely different power when balanced with the higher chakras. Third-chakra power, when balanced, is not in any way negative or bad or to be avoided. It is in fact absolutely essential to the manifestation of balanced spiritual expression. Only when there's a blockage between third- and fourth-chakra energy flows does a problem exist.

You might find it worthwhile to pause a few moments, put the book aside, and reflect on your own feelings concerning all the people you have known both personally and through the media who have packed a big charge of third-chakra willpower and manifested it in various ways. . . . Furthermore, what is your own willpower history . . .

## WILL TRANSFORMED BY LOVE

In exactly the other direction, people with an underactive, blocked energy center will be weak, ineffective, and unable to fully manifest their needs and desires. Most of us fall into this category at least in certain parts of our lives. We have many desires and dreams, but for one reason or another we fail to act in ways that would fulfill them. Kundalini meditation acts to resolve such blocks. However, it should be noted that once we tap into the higher chakras more deeply, our desires and dreams begin to be modified. As we gain a broader view of what life is all about, we alter our plans to accommodate our expanded notion of what we want to do with our lives.

I remember my early twenties very clearly, when I first realized that I seemed to have certain powers, especially in the realm of hypnosis, a vein of psychological research I was working in at the time. My spiritual meditations were waking up an increased flow of kundalini energy through my chakras, and for a time I was tempted to use these powers for third-chakra occult manipulations. The lure of staying down in the lower chakras once kundalini energy is increased is definitely seductive. We would all like to be powerful magicians, able to manipulate all manner of things, but in a balanced kundalini meditation program, such as I was fortunately learning, the desire for occult power becomes transformed in most people by the downflow of heart energy—of love and wisdom from above.

## BLOCKED CHAKRAS

How is it that one or more of our chakras becomes blocked? Are we born this way, is it a matter of our psychological conditioning, or is there some third explanation?

As children, as I mentioned before, we progress through a genetic blueprint for our physical, emotional, and mental development. As a therapist I can state without hesitation that if a child is damaged in the unfolding of one of its basic attributes, this dimension will remain blocked as an adult. This is true of cognitive, emotional, and even sometimes physical development. For instance, if you got hurt in the realms of the heart as a child, your Heart Chakra will remain blocked as an adult—until you face this blockage and risk allowing energy to flow through that chakra again.

I also feel that there is a certain genetic predisposition that influences how our chakras open or fail to open, and at what time in our life this opening takes place. People such as Gopi Krishna place major importance upon the genetic factor. There is also a strong Hindu tradition related to the reincarnation factor.

Another major factor is one's present and past environment, as it offers chances to learn and advance spiritually. By this I mean teachers of all types, including books. I do feel there is a certain magic to life that brings us what we are ready for when we are ready for it, and our challenge is to recognize the lesson and the teacher, and to take advantage of the situation. If we fail to open up and learn, our chakras remain unawakened.

What do you think? To what factors do you attribute your present spiritual condition? If you feel you have blocked chakras, why is this so? And if you have been lucky enough to regularly expand your spiritual capacity for kundalini energy flows, why have you been blessed with this advanced condition? Was it genetic, was it reincarnational, was it a matter of your childhood experiences, or your conscious adult actions?

Take a few moments to tune in to your breathing if you have lost awareness of it while reading . . . become aware of your first chakra . . . your second . . . your third . . . your entire chakra system as a whole now . . . and reflect on the questions that I just raised . . . do you have blocks, and if so, why?

## THE RADIANT GEMSTONE

We are dealing with the sun in this third chakra, so it makes perfect sense that the word for the third chakra is related to that power. In the *Gautamiya-Tantra*, one of the oldest of the scriptures in the *Vaisnava-Tantra* series of Yogic instructions, there is the following statement: "This Lotus [the third chakra] is called Mani-pura because it is lustrous like a gem."

When you meditate upon this chakra, you can envision if you like a radiant red center of energy deep down in your power center.

Red is in fact the primary kundalini color. Sir John Woodroffe says, "Kundalini as a matter of fact should always be meditated upon as red in colour."

However, again I offer words of caution—you will push yourself too fast too soon if you overdo third-chakra meditations in general, and if you overdo the holding of the color red in your mind in particular. Go easy. Make sure the manipulating part of your personality doesn't latch on to the techniques I am giving you for kundalini awakening. There must always be a balance of freedom and spontaneity in spiritual life.

I must confess that in my dealings with Yogic adepts, I have often felt that they tend to be people who are overly fixated in the manipulative powers of their third chakra, often to the detriment of Heart-Chakra awakening. Such a statement might not make me popular in certain extreme circles of Yogic practice, but at the same time, especially as a therapist with much background in working with clients who had spent years of extreme discipline in ashrams before shifting into less controlled lifestyles, I feel honesty is of great value here. There has been too much manipulation of the human spirit through third-chakra control, and too little loving enjoyment of the spiritual path. Kundalini energy is a wild animal, not one that likes to be tamed and tormented by severe and constant control. Instead we should become intimate friends with this energy and participate in its magic, while still leaving it free.

All things in moderation.

## THE WILD RAM

What a curious coincidence we have here, that the sound in Sanskrit for the third chakra is *RAM* and the animal associated with this chakra, in English, is the ram.

I very much like to meditate upon the ram while doing third-chakra expansions. The ram, after all, is great at pushing and is extremely strong for its size. But it is also an animal that has remarkable balance and excellent restraint. The ram also has a very independent spirit, not liking to be dominated and trained. It has its own nature and lives by this nature. Thus, the animal spirit of the third chakra leads us beautifully into the proper way of relating to the third-chakra energies: respect, balance, and harmony with nature.

I encourage you to let the ram-spirit come into you while doing the power-chakra meditations.

## WILLPOWER'S SAVING GRACE: LAUGHTER

Alan Watts, a true ram in many meanings of the word, was the first to teach me that the power center absolutely must have the quality of humor, of laughter, if it is to be activated in a balanced, positive way. Alan was certainly a flawed master, as he himself knew all too well, but he was a great teacher nonetheless. He could laugh beautifully both at himself and at human beings in general who attempted with their intellects to control and define the infinite spiritual realms of life.

In fact, many of the true spiritual Masters of all ages have said that if you are to have great personal power, make sure you have a great laugh to go along with it. If you have read any of the Castaneda books about the Yaqui Indian Master Don Juan Mateus, you know of the remarkable laughing sessions that punctuate Don Juan's teachings. I have known several Zen Masters with a similar laugh. My Sufi teacher in San Francisco in the late sixties, Samuel Lewis, had likewise a remarkable laugh.

All great Masters continually leave the logical realms of consciousness behind and encounter the seeming incongruities that make up the substance of spiritual reality. This is the trick of the Masters— to be able to laugh when the pressure of kundalini realization becomes too great.

It should also become your personal escape valve if you over-charge yourself. Do your best to realize when you are taking yourself too seriously. Remember that life is an infinite heartfelt joke of the Great Guffaw—and we are the ones being tickled; this is the message of laughter in the third chakra.

## ORGANIC INTERNAL-COMBUSTION MACHINES

The third chakra is where the power of combustion comes into action in the human body. This internal human combustion, called digestion, is our way of taking fuel and oxygen and combining them into tiny inner explosions that generate the heat and energy we need to stay alive and active. We are in fact on fire inside, though the fire is remarkably well controlled.

In the first chakra, the chief operating force is gravity. In the second chakra, the chief operating force is the attraction of opposites. In the third chakra, the chief operating force is combustion. In the first two chakras, there exists a power which is felt as a pull. In the third chakra something quite different happens. We have an explosion—a release of energy. It is this release of energy that provides our willpower with the energy to manifest our desires and dreams in the world.

The third chakra, quite expectedly, regulates the functioning of the adrenal glands located in the solar plexus. The adrenals are our source of instant surges of power when we become frightened or angry.

A sluggish set of adrenals, related to a third chakra that is understimulated, will keep us chronically underpowered. Many peo-ple I work with in therapy who are in chronically depressive moods respond beautifully to a gentle program for bringing kundalini energy up into the third chakra. Usually some explosive anger will be related to this kundalini awakening, and this is perfectly fine as a cathartic phase of emotional healing. In conjunction, it is important to encourage a flow of healing energy from the higher chakras so that the third chakra is brought into full equilibrium.

Bringing balance (rather than overstimulation) to the third chakra will help us to maintain an even flow of personal power that we can count on. When equal energy is coming from above as from below, the power center functions beautifully.

The pancreas glands are also intimately related with the third chakra. Our digestion, therefore, will be directly influenced by our third-chakra condition. Many people with digestive disorders need to balance the third chakra for their systems to become efficient combustion machines.

## THE BREATH OF FIRE

In the *Upanishads*, one of the main collections of Yogic instructions from ancient times in India, there is a special kundalini breathing exercise called the Breath of Fire. I will teach you this technique as a direct way of increasing the flow of kundalini energy in your third chakra. Use it at your own discretion, in moderation. "As lions, elephants and tigers are tamed very slowly and cautiously, so should prana [breathing] be brought under control very slowly, in gradation measured according to one's capacity and physical limitations." (This warning is offered in the ancient *Hatha Yoga Pradipika*.)

My feeling is that we definitely should learn to control our breathing by doing several such *pranayama* breathing techniques on a regular basis. When balanced with equal sessions of nonmanipulatory breath-watching meditations, optimum spiritual balance is maintained. The first few breath meditations I have given you have been mostly spontaneous breathing techniques, where you observe your breathing but don't try to control it. In this new breath meditation we are going to temporarily control the breathing in quite a radical pattern.

## The Breath of Fire Meditation

The Breath of Fire meditation is performed with very little air in the lungs. It is the opposite of slow, deep breathing.

(1) Begin with a rapid, powerful contraction of your belly muscles, so that you push air out of your lungs through the mouth almost instantaneously. (This sudden exhale is very similar to how you exhale when coughing, and there should be a slight sound in the throat as the air rushes out. However, the Breath of Fire exhale is different from a cough in that this is a controlled exhale, and centered down in the region of the third chakra, rather than up in the throat. What is most important is that the exhale happen almost instantaneously, with an aggressive power.)

(2) After making such an exhale, relax your breathing muscles completely for a short time (about half a second), so that a very quick inflow of air can happen to replace the air you have discharged. (Again, the coughing inhale is similar to the Breath of Fire inhale, except that in this case, the inhale is smoother, more conscious, and you only make one exhale contraction per breath, where with a hacking cough, you make several belly contractions with each breath cycle.)

(3) Just as soon as air has rushed into your lungs to replace what you had pushed out, again push the air out with a strong, sudden exhale, contracting your diaphragm and abdominal muscles with coughing force. Let the *Huh!* sound come out your throat with each of these exhales, then instantly relax and let air rush in.

The entire cycle of "exhale-inhale" will take you only half a second or so to accomplish. Continue with this way of breathing for perhaps twenty cycles, and advance into more cycles when you feel prepared for a higher charging of your kundalini system. You might find it helpful to count silently to yourself as you do each breath, counting on each power-exhale.

Your sphincter muscle will naturally contract while you do this powerful breathing exercise. In fact, any strenuous physical activity instantly generates sphincter contraction—a reflexive tensing at the bottom of the chakra system to generate instant increase in available energy in the system. With kundalini meditation, we are employing this natural technique of energetic charging for the specific purpose not of gross physical action, but of subtle inner energization.

I recommend that you take time, either now or when convenient in the next few hours, to experiment with this Breath of Fire exercise. It definitely takes practice to master. Quite soon though, you should discover that it is both a natural charging act, and also a very pleasurable one.

Keep in mind that, in a full kundalini meditation session, the Breath of Fire is done after you have done the meditations on the first two chakras. Let me again outline the entire process we have learned thus far so it is perfectly clear in your mind:

(1) First focus on your breathing, heartbeat, balance, whole body here in the present moment.

(2) Then do the sphincter contraction meditation, to center yourself in the first chakra at the base of your spine. (See page 95.)

(3) Do the energy pump breathing next, to bring energy both up and down into your "earthly" first chakra. (See pages 98–99.)

(4) Next, chant the first-chakra mantra, *LAM* or *LANG.*

(5) Next, meditate on the first-chakra mandala. (See pages 100–101.)

(6) Now to focus on the second chakra, do the kundalini-rising breath meditation found on pages 120–121, where you consciously pull energy up into the second chakra with every new inhale.

(7) Hold your attention in your genital area as you breathe, and open yourself to the awakening of this "liquid" chakra.

(8) Do the second chakra vocal meditation (mantra) which is *VAM* or *VANG*.

(9) Meditate upon the visual meditation (mandala).

(10) Now to advance into third-chakra focusing, do the Breath of Fire breathing meditation we just learned.

## THIRD-CHAKRA MENTAL FOCUSING

The Breath of Fire breathing meditation will powerfully move your attention to the third chakra region of your body. After finishing a Breath of Fire meditation, sit quietly, observe your breathing at rest, and focus on the movement of your belly as you breathe.

The following focusing meditation will enable you to amplify your awareness of the presence of the third chakra.

As you exhale, contract your belly muscles until you're completely empty of air. . . . Hold on empty for a while until you feel a growing pressure to inhale. (This pressure, combined with the tension in your belly muscles, will point your attention directly to your third chakra.)

Now inhale through the nose quickly, letting your lungs fill up with air while your attention remains focused on your belly . . .

Exhale again as before, contracting your abdomen

muscles slowly until you are completely empty and hungering for air . . .

Inhale again quickly and continue with this pattern until you feel deeply centered in your third, "fire" chakra . . .

## THIRD-CHAKRA VOCAL AWAKENING

Now that you have advanced your attention to the third chakra and awakened this center with a breathing meditation, it is time to employ vocalization to further awaken and balance the chakra.

The sound of the third chakra is *RAM* or if you prefer, *RANG*. As you sit in quiet meditation on the third chakra, begin to allow this sound to manifest effortlessly from your inner being. First just hear it slightly in your mind, as the *Rrrrr* generates power and volume deep within your third-chakra region. There is great power in this *Rrrrr* sound. Open yourself to it—the universe will join you in your calling on third-chakra energization.

Make sure you let your breathing pace your chanting, even when it is first silent chanting, deep within you. The sound emerges on your exhales as an active expression. On your inhales, the sound resonates within you even when you are not actively generating it. Then comes the next natural exhale, and the sound grows in intensity, beginning to vibrate in your vocal system, until it finally manifests as auditory sound projected into the outside world.

You will notice that the beginning consonant of the chant generates the primal pressure, then as you advance to the *am* or *ang* ending, this sound releases the power of the consonant with a gentle explosion. Enjoy this experience, and let yourself go deeper and deeper into free expression of the primal sound. Keep the sound at a level where you feel rising power, but don't push into a forced, aggressive sound. What you are learning is how to "sit" on an increased charge of personal power, to enjoy this charge, and to then move it up into the heart chakra.

## THE THIRD-CHAKRA POWER MANDALA

Zachary has developed one of the best third-chakra illustrations I have ever encountered, either in ancient texts or contemporary renderings. Let me again offer you a description and explanation of the mandala. Then you can turn to the insert and experience the mandala meditation for yourself.

Zachary has placed a red triangle in the center of the mandala, as is traditionally done. The triangle represents fire, and also the triumvirate relationship of the three lower chakras, which together make up the basic human foundation for survival and spiritual growth.

Then around the circle of white that encompasses the triangle he has painted the ten lotus buds, in alternating red and green. The fiery red is normal for the third chakra, but the green color is unconventional. When I first looked at this mandala I was bothered—after all, the color green is supposed to be the color of the fourth, Heart Chakra, not involved in the third at all.

But then with my first meditation upon this mandala, I immediately experienced what Zachary was doing—even while focusing on the third chakra, he was bringing our attention effortlessly and helpfully up toward the fourth chakra. The red petals move our attention down and back to the origins of the kundalini energy, so that we keep a good flow moving in that direction, and the green petals move us upward toward the Heart Chakra.

In this way, through meditating on this mandala, we are not overpowered by the redness of the sun, and the source of the rising kundalini energy from down below. Instead we experience a radiating movement up into the heart, into compassion, into an integration of will and love.

This movement from third-chakra to fourth-chakra awareness is a primary theme for our times, as we have seen. Brilliant therapists, such as Rollo May in his book *Love and Will*, have addressed this topic from a psychological point of view in recent decades. What we are doing is learning concrete and powerful meditations that directly affect the balance that many people have spoken about theoretically.

Each time you look meditatively at this third-chakra mandala, you will in effect be giving yourself the therapy session that our whole civilization hungers for—the balancing of aggressive masculine will-power with loving, more feminine compassion.

As you turn to meditate perhaps for the first time on this third-chakra mandala, remember to go through the preliminary procedures you have learned. Become aware of your breathing . . . your first chakra . . . second chakra . . . third chakra . . . vibrate with the *RAM* or *RANG* chant. . . . Look at the mandala as you have learned before, taking it in through the four different ways of seeing . . . movement . . . shape . . . color . . . space . . . and open yourself to a spontaneous meditative experience as you move a new step into kundalini consciousness.

# 8

# Radiating Compassion
# (Fourth Chakra)

*We now come to* the chakra associated with the presence of a magical quality we call love, which ideally serves as the underpinning of all the other chakra qualities of the human energetic system.

It should be noted that human love never stands on its own—it is empowered by the energetic interplays of the first three chakras. As we will see clearly once we have progressed through all seven of the energy centers of the human body, human love is actually generated by the merging of energy from the top three chakras with energy from the bottom three. When there is an ample flow of energy both from above and from below, the Heart Chakra is radiant, balanced, and healthy.

Below the Heart Chakra, as we have seen, lies the world of matter, of survival and procreation, of manipulation and mastery over the physical realms of life. Above lies the world of spirit, of pure thought and intuition, of interpersonal communication and, ultimately, universal unity and transcendence.

The Heart Chakra, in its most basic sense, is the marriage of matter and spirit, of concrete and abstract, of knowledge and wisdom, of earth and heaven. It lies at the center, and when balanced with energies from above and below, serves as the true location of the creative force of the universe in the human body.

You will remember that the Heart Chakra is considered feminine. It interacts with the equal and opposite masculine chakra just below it, transforming third-chakra ego power into a totally new level of consciousness—that of compassionate and powerful love. The ability to let go of selfish desires and make personal sacrifices to help other human beings is generated by the awakening of the fourth chakra.

The transformational vortex of the fourth chakra also serves to take the sexual energy from the second chakra, which as we saw is also a feminine energy center, and transmute this raw desire to mate into a higher level. The energy of the second chakra bonds with the energy of the higher-frequency fourth chakra so that love can come into being at the very center of sexual passion.

## MERGING POWER AND LOVE

As I hinted at before, human love requires willpower in order to manifest. Love as a philosophical or theological concept is one thing. Love that can act in the world, which can express itself in compassionate interaction with other human beings, needs a great deal of power to overcome the inertia of habitual self-centered behavioral and emotional patterns. Love transforms will, and will empowers love. This interaction of these two polarities is one of the most beautiful dynamics of our chakratic system.

Willpower, when aimed upward instead of allowed to flow downward into sexual obsession and manipulation, overcomes intervening obstacles and leads us to our fourth chakra. According to Joseph Chilton Pearce, "The third chakra uses willpower to unite the second chakra with the fourth, unifying sex and love."

A great deal of a therapist's time is spent in helping people to succeed in making this step. So many people, men in particular, are trapped like psychic prisoners in the dominance of their lower three chakras, with perhaps their fifth thinking chakra also being hyperactive, but their fourth, Heart Chakra, is defunct, seemingly kaput, habitually blocked against coming into active participation with the other chakras.

In the seventies many men attempted to escape from their non-compassionate, aggressive masculine habits, and to move into their more feminine loving qualities, through trying to block their inherent willpower and tendency to dominate—that is, by blocking their third-chakra expressions. Men were led to believe that by becoming soft and submissive they could attain higher levels of spiritual realization and establish better relationships with the opposite sex.

This has proved ultimately not to be the case. Instead, these men found themselves slipping back into infantile, first- and second-chakra levels of energy, perhaps able to resonate with needy, soft feelings, but lacking the firepower to break through their emotional weaknesses and emerge into genuine compassionate dimensions of loving.

The message of kundalini wisdom is that willpower should not be subjugated. It should be used to its fullest. But it should be put to use in upward-rising energy flows, not in downward-spiraling mani-festations. Ultimately it takes willpower to empower the Heart Chakra. We must never forget this.

One of the reasons I find the kundalini approach to personal growth ideal is that it offers concrete techniques for doing certain things that other philosophies, religions, and therapy techniques only talk about. It's fine and dandy to speak great words about merging will and love, for instance, but how can we do this in practice? What are the actual steps to take to transform our lower energy centers with the power of love found in the Heart Chakra?

## LOCATING THE CENTER

The first obvious step is to determine where our spiritual heart center, our fourth chakra, is located in our bodies. The Christian cross offers a perfect way to locate this center. All you have to do is to raise your arms out to each side and tune experientially in to the point where the vertical intersects with the horizontal. There you have your heart center. It is little wonder that the Christian faith, where love is equated with God, found this cross image to express the heart of the Christian message. I suggest that you pause and actually explore this simple and yet perfectly centering cross meditation—which I learned many years ago from a radical and very loving professor at the San Francisco Theological Seminary.

After reading this paragraph, put the book aside a moment. . . .

> Tune in to your breathing as usual, close your eyes perhaps, and raise both arms out to form a cross . . . breathe . . . feel the power of this posture not as a religious symbol, but as an experiential awakening of your Heart Chakra—as energies from below and above come together and begin that remarkable fourth-chakra swirling that generates love in the center of the human body. . . .

## PRANA: THE ULTIMATE STUFF OF LIFE

*Prana* is another potent Sanskrit word that conveys an absolutely fundamental dimension of human life. I do not want to turn this word and concept into an idol to worship, as so many people have. But I do want to offer you a solid grounding in *prana* consciousness.

*Prana* has been described as "a homogeneous unity present in every part of the body. It is the subtle, invisible, all-pervading, divine energy of eternal life. Invisible in itself, its operations are manifest. It determines the birth, growth and decay of all animated organisms."

The *Upanishads*, the Tantra scriptures, the *Raghava-Bhatta* texts from ancient times, as well as many contemporary books, abound in glorious and often contradictory descriptions of the ultimate qualities of *prana*. I prefer to maintain a more experiential approach to *prana*, by seeing this underlying energetic force first and foremost as the air we breathe.

We have moved through the elements of earth, water, and fire. Now we come to the fourth element, air. Note that there is no fire without air, no combustion without oxygen. Likewise there is no fire without the earth element carbon. We can see clearly that the third chakra, fire, is fueled both from below (carbon) and above (air), to generate the heat and energy of fire.

In ancient times, the spiritual Masters knew from direct inner revelation that each breath, and the air taken in with each breath, was somehow magical, determining the quality of life and vitality in each individual. It was therefore postulated that the air must hold a magical, life-giving substance, which they called *prana*.

Much later, just a hundred or so years ago, in all our third-chakra scientific glory, we discovered in fact that the air we breathe has in it a magical substance called oxygen, which as far as we can tell does fuel our every moment of life on this planet.

But notice what popular science tends to do. It makes a discovery, such as the presence of oxygen in the atmosphere, then claims that the mystery is over, that everything has been explained—that there is no *prana* after all, no mystic substance beyond human comprehension. Everything is explained by labeling the mysterious substance with the name "oxygen."

But what is oxygen?

My professor friend at the University of Zurich gives the latest scientific answer to this question—we simply don't know what oxygen is. We know some of its properties. But the deeper we look into subatomic activities, the less we really understand of the underlying reality of the air we breathe. The mystery becomes bigger as our scientific knowledge grows more massive. *Prana* remains a great mystery, which science cannot fathom to its ultimate depths, but which human beings can make direct contact with through meditation.

Each time we inhale, we are taking into our body *prana*, which the scientists label by the deductive term "oxygen." This energy source enters our body, then interacts chemically to produce combustion, which gives us the power to continue functioning at cellular levels.

We will never know the ultimate mystery of how this works, no matter how sophisticated our third-chakra/fifth-chakra explanation of scientific processes might become. But we can learn to look directly inward to experience this process at work. We can use the microscope of consciousness itself to catch *prana* in action. This is a remarkably exciting thing to do! Why do so few people regularly do it?

The answer to that question is more simple than one might suspect. We are afraid to look inward and directly encounter our spiritual nature, our experiential functioning, because to do so we must let go of all our old concepts. We must transcend the third chakra to attain the fourth. We must give up our manipulative control of the environment and our conceptual grasp on reality if we are to look with whole eyes inward and see intuitively the process of life in action.

*Prana* can in fact be observed in action. This is what breath watching is all about. But the thinking mind must become quiet for the observation to happen. This is what is almost impossible for many people to do—especially those caught up in third-chakra games of dominance and intellectual superiority.

Meditation is the technique through which we learn to put aside our concepts, our manipulating mental tools, for at least long enough to gain a fleeting glimpse of a magnitude of consciousness far beyond the third-chakra dimension of deductive reasoning.

We must surrender our cognitive guns at the door of meditational insight, if we are to enter the realms of kundalini consciousness.

Are you ready?

## PRANAYAMA BREATHING

I want to teach you at this point one of the main breath exercises of the ancient *pranayama* discipline. The great Yoga teacher Patanjali taught this breathing technique in his writings several thousand years ago. The technique remains as new and powerful as it was when he was instructing his students in its practice then.

There are two equal-and-opposite ways to do this breath meditation, and I highly recommend that you always do both when you do either, so that your breathing becomes balanced in the Heart Chakra. With one way, your breathing will raise your conscious attention upward into your head, so that heart and head become unified. In breathing the opposite way, you will move your consciousness down deeply into your lower three chakras, to unify them with the heart energy.

The pattern is extremely easy to learn to do once you understand the principle involved. This is the breathing vehicle for the fourth chakra, and it stands as one of the primary kundalini meditations.

Try the alternate-nostril breathing pattern (on pages 154–155) on your own for perhaps eight to twelve cycles, and experience for yourself how this breathing calms you, balances the lower chakras, and brings energy throughout your system.

## THE HEART CHANT

You now know how to locate your Heart Chakra (the arms-out cross meditation) and how to circulate heart energy through the chakra system through the alternate-nostril breathing you just learned. We are ready at this point to learn the third vehicle for waking up this energy center: the vocalization of the mantra for the fourth chakra.

Before introducing this sound to you, let me mention that these

■■■■■■■■■■■■■■■■■■■■■■■■■■■■

## Alternate-Nostril Breathing

(1) Sit comfortably, and turn your attention to your free breathing for at least a minute or two before you begin to control the breathing at all. . . . If you wish, move your arms out to each side to form the cross, to bring your attention directly to your fourth-chakra center. . . .

(2) Now raise one of your hands to your nose, palm facing your mouth, and put your thumb beside one nostril and your forefinger beside the other, so that you can easily close one air passage or the other through slight pressure on the nose. . . .

(3) First, to move your breathing attention deep down into your first three chakras to balance these chakras and charge them with a downflow of loving energy from above, simply close the nostril on the thumb side by pushing gently against the nose on that side, while you slowly exhale through the other nostril. . . .

(4) At the bottom of your exhale, be empty a moment, as you focus deep down even into the earth below your first chakra . . . then release the thumb from the nose

basic sounds can be held in your mind throughout the day as an underlying spiritual music for whatever you are doing. I often bring the Heart-Chakra music to being in my mind, for instance. Or, when I want more power in my life, I bring the third-chakra music into my background consciousness. And when I am entering into sexual relating, I often begin by bringing the second-chakra chant into my inner realms of consciousness. Likewise, when I need to ground into and press with the forefinger on the other side of the nose so that you inhale through the other nostril. . . .

(5) At the top of this inhale, keep your fingers the same as on the inhale, and exhale through the same nostril until you are empty of air. . . . Hold on empty. . . .

(6) Now reverse the nostril pressure so that when you inhale, you inhale through the other nostril . . . hold a moment at the top of the inhale, then exhale through the same nostril . . . now switch nostrils for a full inhale-exhale cycle . . . switch again for the next inhale-exhale cycle . . . switch again. . . .

(7) Continue with this pattern, where you inhale and exhale on one side, then switch and inhale and exhale on the other side. . . .

(8) Inhale fully—don't switch nostrils—exhale completely.

Now switch nostrils—inhale—exhale.

Switch nostrils—inhale—exhale.

Switch nostrils—inhale—exhale.

And continue. . . .

---

the Earth, I willfully resonate with the first-chakra chant. When I want to expand into the realm of communication, I let the fifth-chakra music come into my mind as background resonance. Finally, when I'm in deep meditation, the *OM* of the sixth chakra often fills my mind. You are encouraged to do likewise.

What I hope you are starting to feel for yourself is that each of the different chakra sounds creates a vibrational experience directly in

## Heart Consciousness Rising

To reverse the breath exercise, the trick to remember is that you want to make the switch between nostrils at the top of your inhales (to stimulate heart-head integration), as opposed to making the switch at the bottom of your exhales (to stimulate heart-torso integration).

With the reversed breathing pattern, you are going to bring energy/*prana* up into your head with every inhale. Hold on full breath for a moment, then switch to the other nostril as you exhale. Inhale on the same side, bringing more energy up to the head. Then switch over to the other nostril for the next exhale-inhale cycle.

Try this head-heart breathing for yourself now, following the simple pattern of:

Exhale—don't switch nostrils—inhale.
Now switch nostrils—exhale—inhale.
Switch—exhale—inhale.
And continue. . . .

the region of the chakra associated with it. No scientific explanation has yet been developed for why the particular consonant associated with each chakra stimulates a vibrational experience in that chakra, but this is what does happen. Thus the actual sound of a chakra will help your mind to focus on that chakra.

We are now ready to welcome the mantra of the fourth chakra into the symphony of chakratic sounds. The sound is a soft feminine *YAM* or *YANG*.

Take plenty of time to experience this special heart sound . . . sit quietly, and allow your breathing to come and go of itself, with no effort to alter it . . . notice how your breathing relaxes on its own when you turn your attention to it . . . expand your awareness to include your whole-body presence . . . feel energy flowing into your chakra system both from above and from below . . . extend your arms out to each side to bring your attention to your Heart Chakra. . . .

Now begin to let the heart mantra, *YAM* or *YANG*, come alive inside you, beginning with a very soft *Y* quality, which is actually best represented as a gentle *Eeeeeeeeey* sound . . . and halfway through your exhalation, move into the second part of the sound, which is the same for all the chakra mantras, the *Aaaaaah* sound in the middle of the mantra . . . then finish with the choice of *Mmmmmm* or *Nnnngggggggg*. . . .

## ANAHATA, OR LETTING GO

The Sanskrit name for the Heart Chakra is a curious one, superficially meaning "unstruck," "unhurt," "bright," "clean." Deeper into the sacred meaning of this word, we find that *anahata* means "the sound that is created without any two things striking." In the ancient writings of the Yogic Master Visvanatha, it is said that in the Heart Chakra we discover "the sound which is Sabda-brahmamaya, which is produced by no cause."

Again I think of discussions with my physicist friend Eduard Cartier, who finds this notion of a sound being generated without any known source to be extremely sympathetic to certain theories in astrophysics about the origins of the universe.

The key point to establish here is that in the intuitive understanding of Yogic tradition there exists at the very center of each chakra a nucleus called the seed, or the *bija*. From this seed emanates a vibration, which is both a sound and also an essential energy pattern that governs that particular chakra.

The nucleus of each chakra was understood by the Yogic Masters to be the energetic programming that controls the development of the part of the body under the influence of that chakra. Thus we find that thousands of years ago, the Hindu tradition intuitively comprehended the genetic basis of life. This comprehension came not from scientific experimentation but from inner looking to the core of life—to the *bija*.

It is essential to remember during fourth-chakra meditations that the Heart Chakra is called by the name of *anahata*, the *bija* sound that comes from nowhere, that is not created by known means, that originates from the void and manifests in the Heart Chakra. I mentioned earlier that in the Sanskrit understanding of life, sound vibration is considered to be the originating power of the universe. Everything that exists is made up of sound vibration. Such a vision of the universe is, again, in perfect resonance with the new physics as popularized by such scientific writers as Fritjof Capra, Gary Zukav, and Itzhak Bentov.

Thus when you chant the *bija*-mantra for each of the chakras, you are doing something that is truly amazing. You are tuning your entire physical and mental being to the exact sound of the chakra you are chanting and aligning yourself with the mysterious center of your chakratic universe.

Let me mention that scientists are presently struggling with the significance of a new discovery about the massive galaxies that make up the known universe. It was always assumed that these galaxies would be randomly distributed throughout the universe. But in fact, recent analysis indicates that they are organized in definite patterns, the meaning of which has not yet been determined.

For me this is a vital discovery of science. I consider our personal chakras to be galaxies. "As within, so without." When we look deeply into the innards of an atom, we come across galaxies of spinning vortexes that defy deeper penetration, at least at this point in scientific exploration. And as we look to our personal chakras, we discover the same thing: vast universes that become yet vaster the more we look in their direction.

We are looking at infinite inner galaxies when we turn our attention to any of the chakras within our own bodies. In fact, as Rodney Collin shows in *The Theory of Celestial Influence*, our energetic bodies are nothing less than a tiny microcosm of the universe as a whole.

This is such a vast notion that we surely should not take it too seriously. Instead we should laugh great guffaws when we momentarily glimpse the chakratic galaxies within us. What a joke, that we think ourselves such small unimportant entities, when in fact we contain at least seven galaxies of infinite dimensions within us. No wonder Alan Watts would often look into my eyes, and burst out laughing at the seriousness on my face as I considered my tiny ego concerns in the face of the galactic reality of my chakratic presence.

To chant the *bija*-mantra of your Heart Chakra is to focus your mind's attention directly to the center of that central galaxy that swirls within you. What a daring thing to do! And yet, in practice, what a calming, balancing, centering thing to do. You are that galaxy, after all. It is you. You are simply expanding your consciousness so as to become a participating part of the infinite whole.

This, in essence, is what meditation is all about.

With such notions swirling within the vortex of your consciousness, see what experience comes to you if you leave your concepts at the celestial gate, and enter into the *anahata* chant . . . breathe with complete freedom . . . eyes closed perhaps . . . center yourself in your chakra system of swirling galaxies . . . and set yourself vibrating with the heart-sound that originates beyond everything you know . . . *YAM.* . . .
*YANG.* . . .

## VISION OF THE HEART
## (FOURTH-CHAKRA MANDALA)

Zachary has done something quite daring with his fourth-chakra mandala painting. Normally, in the popular texts, the fourth chakra is done up in greens, since this is considered to be the color of the heart. But Zachary has transformed the somewhat static presentation of the Heart Chakra into a more dynamic experience, as you will soon discover for yourself.

You will remember that in the third chakra, he used the color green to point you toward the fourth chakra. Now as you arrive at the fourth chakra, the *anahata* energy center, you find not the "outer," green energy of this chakra, but what is described in the ancient texts as the "inner" *bija* color of the *anahata* chakra—gold!

"Here dwells Kakini [the inner goddess of the fourth chakra], who in colour is yellow like unto new lightning, exhilarated and auspicious," according to a Sanskrit text quoted by perhaps the top traditional scholar of kundalini, Sir John Woodroffe, in his 1918 translation of the kundalini scriptures. "This Linga [goddess] is like shining gold, like the steady tapering flame of a candle in a windless place." What an image for the Heart Chakra!

When you meditate on Zachary's mandala, you will discover a six-pointed star created by two triangles, called *trikonas* in Sanskrit. Such triangles are associated with several of the chakras, as Zachary has shown, but it is in the Heart Chakra that the triangle form is most strongly presented, made double so as to generate six smaller triangles aiming out in all directions, sending the *anahata bija*–vibration out to the other six chakras. The image is perfect.

Each of the six chakra-triangles then generates two lotus petals—one to penetrate and awaken the lower physical chakras and one to penetrate and awaken the higher spiritual dimensions of life.

When you look to the center of this mandala, breathe, and let your mind surrender to a nonconceptual experience, you do look directly to the center of your own universe. We have in many crucial ways arrived at the centerpoint, here in the Heart Chakra. I consider it vital to keep this primary mandala in mind most frequently, so that the *bija*-sound can regularly be called upon, from the center of the universe, even from beyond the universe, to enter your personal life and energize all your chakras in a balanced way.

Kundalini packs an ultimate wallop, which is why we are devoting such an intimate focus of attention to its total configuration. Remember, when it becomes too much, let the Great Guffaw break forth so that you don't take any of this too seriously.

Sometimes when you are looking at the center of a mandala, you might find yourself "seeing things." For instance, with the fourth-chakra mandala you might see faces of people you love. You might also see a face of someone you don't know, a Master coming to you. Be open to such visions, although it is best not to hold on to them, as we shall see in more detail with the fifth chakra.

The fourth chakra's animal spirit, by the way, is an antelope or deer, a strong yet sensitive, high-bounding yet earth-centered animal. Sometimes this animal might come to you while doing the fourth-chakra mandala meditation. The spirit of this animal can bring you closer to your own heart spirit. Breathe and enjoy this antelope-energy coming into you. . . .

I could wax poetic on the basic theme of the centrality of the Heart Chakra. But instead, let me fall silent, let words pass away, so that you can turn to the heart mandala, do the full meditation as you have perhaps learned by heart by now, and open yourself to a new experience, to a new contact with the divine within . . . listen to the sound that emanates from the very center of the *anahata* mandala, even while you are quietly chanting the sound of the *anahata*. . . .

# 9

# Kundalini in Action
# (Fifth Chakra)

*Virtually all human communication* is based strongly within the fifth energy center, which we are going to explore in this chapter. For instance, every moment I have been writing this book and communicating through these words to you, I have been employing a great deal of power from the fifth chakra, since this is the chakra of interpersonal communication. Without it there would be no interchange of ideas from one person to another, and virtually no human civilization at all.

It makes perfect sense for the Communication Chakra to be in the throat region of the body, since this is where our basic communication tool is located—the larynx. Through this remarkable organ we are able to take the outflow of air through our windpipe, and transform the rushing air into a vibratory message for the outside world to pick up and respond to.

The fifth chakra also involves our tongue, mouth, and lips. All these combined, with some help from the third-chakra diaphragm muscle that provides the willpower for expression, constitute the mechanical apparatus needed for vocal communication. We should remember that up until a few hundred years ago, with the invention of the printing press, the vast majority of human communication happened through vocal exchange.

The fifth chakra is also intimately associated with the parts of the brain that generate complex thought flows that end up manifesting through words and deeds. We find ourselves entering the realm of abstract concepts with this chakra.

My experience as a therapist has been that most people in our society are fixated a great deal in the fifth chakra, living in the world of concepts, thoughts, ideas, dreams, and fantasies. We often drop down to the third chakra for the actual energy to manifest our ideas when it comes time for action. And we shift into second-chakra/fourth-chakra activity when we become sexually aroused or emotionally charged.

But for most of our moment-to-moment existence, we do tend to be lost in thought, to be caught up in words, images, symbols—in the fifth-chakra world of conceptual consciousness.

This is neither good nor bad. It is simply a question of balance. In this chapter we must ask ourselves—are we spending too much or too little time in this chakra, as opposed to the others? Is this chakra dormant, balanced, or hyperactive?

When the Communication Chakra is dormant, we are mentally asleep at the wheel, not thinking things through adequately in order to lead a productive, satisfying life. There are certainly people who are blocked in their analytical, conceptual functioning. When the Communication Chakra is underactive, people tend to be shut off from human interaction, out of the flow of everyday verbal intercourse.

When the Communication Chakra is overactive, that energy is drained from the other chakras. For instance, most of us get caught up in the habit of thinking-thinking-thinking without tuning in to our Heart Chakra enough. Many people also tend to lose contact with the Power Chakra. They become great thinkers but ineffective doers. Many of us also run away from our sexual energies, from the primal source of our kundalini energy, by remaining lost in thought all the time. Head trippers are not known to be great lovers.

The fifth chakra is often out of balance when there isn't adequate downflow from the upper two, more intuitive, spiritual chakras. Unfortunately, we live in a culture that deconditions children from bringing spiritual insight into their cognitive experiences. There is a strong push to unite the fifth chakra with its masculine counterpart down in the third, Power Chakra. But have we ever once taken a course in school that encouraged us to open up to spiritual flows of inspiration from above?

We have made a great error in our interpretation of the American Constitution in this regard. We have assumed that religion and sixth-chakra spiritual intuition are the same, and thus have thrown out the baby with the bathwater. We have kept spiritual, intuitive education out of our schools at the same time that we have kept out dogmatic religious indoctrination.

The result is a nation highly skilled in cognitive activity and in cognitive/manipulative action, but utterly unschooled in intuitive/cognitive mental functionings. We have fixated on the lower masculine chakras and utterly ignored the two highest chakras—and also the central, Heart Chakra. As a result, we tend to be intellectually and physically adept, and spiritually and emotionally inept.

I do not mean in any way to demean our fifth-chakra development. What we have done in the field of communication is absolutely remarkable. I can sit here and almost effortlessly transmit my inner thoughts into the memory of my computer, and you can sit there reading these words in your book, as if we are communicating in the present moment together. Just the printed word in itself, manifesting vocal folklore into solid format, was a radical step for humankind.

My challenge while writing this book, however, has been to consciously maintain my center of awareness not in my fifth chakra, but deeper down in my Heart Chakra and the lower three, as well as higher in the upper two. The last thing in the world you need, from a kundalini point of view, is more input on a purely intellectual level. Getting lost in head trips about the chakras has been a chronic

Western problem, as the wisdom and power of kundalini has spread into our culture.

The chakras, as we have seen, might be represented by concepts, but they are not concepts. They are actual realities. Thus, I have been using concepts as a vehicle for turning your experiential attention away from concepts and toward the reality that lies behind the concepts. How well have I been doing? Are your chakras more than ideas in your head at this point? Are you becoming intimate friends with them as living vibrational entities at the center of your consciousness?

Pause a moment, and let yourself consider this question: Are your chakras real, or are they just figments of your conceptual mind? Have you opened yourself to the actual presence of these mysterious energy vortexes in your body, or have you kept yourself safely locked up in your fifth-chakra intellectual-reflection mode of consciousness?

## VIBRATION HEADQUARTERS

As we have seen, each of the seven chakras is a vibrating energy center that transmits a primal *bija* sound. These are internal vibrations that might spread a certain distance directly. But we require the fifth-chakra communications center if we want to spread our inner feelings and thoughts, our inspired realizations and our singing energies, out into the world around us to be received by other human beings.

Thus, the fifth chakra is a bridge chakra. It moves our inside vibrations forth into the outside world. It provides our primary vehicle for self-expression. The Heart Chakra was the epiphany of our inner-reflective consciousness. We can achieve a perfect sense of balance within ourselves through balancing the Heart Chakra. But in most cases, to connect with the outside world we must rise up into the Throat Chakra to express our feelings, insights, and thoughts.

The fifth chakra is our vehicle for transcending physical reality, for breaking beyond the bounds of touch, of physical manipulation. Through the Throat Chakra we shift into the invisible realm of sound transmission, into the nonphysical dimensions of life. We move beyond our physical self when we start broadcasting ourselves in vibratory form through talking, shouting, singing, and by extension through typing, tape recordings, video, and all the media extensions of our personal bodies.

Long ago it was assumed that there existed a fifth element beyond the four obvious ones of earth, water, fire, and air. This fifth element was called ether in Western terminology, and *akasha* in Sanskrit. This fifth element was where the realms of the spirit were said to reside.

Sound was traditionally associated with this fifth element. The Hindus felt that sound was the primordial origin of all material reality, and as we saw, the ancient Hebrew and Christian placing of the "Word" at the center of material creation reflected this notion that sound existed in a dimension beyond the four elements.

Opening the fifth chakra thus becomes a double process. On one hand, we are opening ourselves to send out into the world our inner experiences, through our organic communication channels and their multitude of subsidiaries in the electronic age. We are also opening ourselves to whatever dimensions exist in the nonphysical realms of consciousness, so that these dimensions can come and communicate with us. In short, the fifth chakra is where we open to the inflow of spiritual communication from above, from the sixth and seventh chakras—which means from the entire spiritual universe.

Carlos Castaneda has written extensively of going into the fifth-chakra astral level of spiritual consciousness and experiencing remarkable and sometimes frightening parallel universes. I myself have also had a number of such "out-of-the-body" experiences. These experiences took me beyond the confines of my physical body. I do not question their validity on some plane of existence. Even regular dreams seem to take us into this fifth-chakra dimension where we are displaced one step from physical reality.

But as Joseph Chilton Pearce clearly states, as a reflection of the spiritual teacher Muktananda's observations, "No experience in this fifth chakra is a mystical experience of God, though it be awesome and paradisaical. The fifth chakra and its possibilities must be conceptualized, and God is not a concept."

So at the lower level of fifth-chakra functioning, we have vocalization and the transmission of concepts through sound vibration and related media transmissions. In the more esoteric dimensions of fifth-chakra experience, we encounter the magical and sometimes horrifying dimension where dreams seem to be real, where ghosts leap out at us and challenge us to call them figments of our hyperactive imaginations, and where visions even of God come to us to inspire our spiritual lives.

I have worked with many clients over the years who were fixated in the astral dimensions of the fifth chakra, and my treatment was always the same—to help them wake up their sixth and fourth chakras, so as to gain more balance between the masculine energies of the Throat Chakra and the feminine energies of the intuitive and Heart Chakras. This is a seemingly pat intellectual answer to what can be very serious psychological problems associated with fifth-chakra hyperactivity. But when we put to use the kundalini vehicles that we have been learning in this book, the treatment becomes concrete and effective.

However, these are considerations of extremes. Mostly I want to focus on the magical middle spectrum in our lives, where we are balanced most of the time and need mainly to fine-tune our chakra energies, not do a major overhaul of the system.

## Using Sound for Purification and Healing

The Sanskrit word for the Throat Chakra is *visuddha*, which literally means "purification." In the Hindu tradition, sound is seen as a purifier. It has the ability to penetrate absolutely everything, and to set everything it penetrates into vibration. In many deep spiritual traditions, sickness was seen as a lack of vibratory vitality or an improper vibration in an organ. And sound therapy in one form or another has been used almost universally to generate a more healthy condition in the body.

There is a great deal of truth to this understanding of sickness and healing as seen by ancient wise men and women throughout the world, as I explored in detail in *Conscious Healing*. Sick people do tend to have flat, inharmonious voices, and to possess serious imbalances in their vibratory habits at chakra levels as well as everyday levels. Constrictions in the Throat Chakra when talking will usually reflect constrictions throughout the chakra system.

In using the vocalization power of the body—chanting the sounds I am teaching you and in general singing and speaking harmoniously—we can directly act to heal ourselves of imbalances at subtle levels of health. Both for mental and physical healing, and for emotional and spiritual healing as well, we can readily tap into the magic of harmonious vibrations.

People who are physically sick, for instance, are usually shut down in the Throat Chakra, and if they want to heal, it is good to gently awaken healthy vibrations through the fifth chakra. It is important, of course, to make sure to regularly balance the chakra system when chanting to regain health. Homeostasis is the aim, not overstimulation of one particular chakra that supposedly controls the health of a particular region of the body.

As a breathing meditation for this fifth chakra, let me share with you the most basic healing chant. This exercise is very simple, yet it can have the most profound effects. It can be done throughout the day, regardless of where you are or what you're doing. It requires no focusing; it has no symbolic meaning. It is the pure power of sound manifesting in your body.

## Humming Meditation

(1) Sit quietly and watch your breaths coming and going, as you would sit and watch the waves coming and going at the beach, each one different but every one similar to the others. . . .

(2) Listen as I taught you before to the sounds being made by your breathing, the subtle vibrations created by the rush of air in and out of your nose. . . .

(3) Very gently, as softly as possible, begin to allow your vocal cords to vibrate as you exhale, generating a quiet humming sound with your lips closed, and your eyes closed as well. . . .

(4) At the bottom of your exhale, fall naturally silent, and as you inhale silently, feel the vibrations continuing throughout your body from your humming a moment before. . . .

(5) Continue with this humming meditation for a number of breaths until you feel that you are becoming sound yourself. . . .

(6) Then be quiet while you continue breathing, and allow the vibrations in your body to remain in your consciousness so that you are listening to every cell and every chakra. . . .

## SYMPATHETIC VIBRATIONS

A remarkable natural tendency of all entities in the universe is to seek harmony with each other—so the scientists say, and the ancient Masters as well. In physics the tendency of two vibrational sources to resonate at the same or harmonic vibrations is called "entrainment." If two strings are vibrating at similar frequencies, for instance, they will soon start vibrating at the same frequency, or a higher or lower harmonic to each other. The pendulums of two clocks ticking just out of phase will also entrain to each other at some point. This is a natural law of vibration, and it carries great import for all of life.

First, it means that people can seek, through various forms of communication, to share a common understanding, a harmonious vision of life—and find it! This is what is supposed to happen with couples living together. They come from disparate backgrounds usually, and have differing emotional and conceptual vibrations to start out with. But the more they live together, if they indeed surrender to the tendency of entrainment, the more they come into a harmonious relationship.

By another of the laws of entrainment, when two vibratory sources merge as one unified vibration, the amplitude, the power of this vibration, becomes greater. Joining forces therefore increases our ability to spread the good news and to hold our own in difficult, disharmonious times. It was Benjamin Franklin, an early American patriot, who pointed out "We must all hang together, else we shall all hang separately."

Thus, families and communities, and hopefully by extension nations and planets, can come to share a harmonious feeling, and also to amplify their positive vibes. If not, there is really no hope for peace, for understanding, for spiritual sharing and creative compassion.

But this sympathetic vibration, this resonance, as it is also called, must first be found within our own systems, within our bodies and our chakras, if it is to manifest and entrain with others. If our own vibratory system is disharmonious, if our chakras are fighting against each other and not surrendering to the entrainment principle, then everywhere we go we will spread this disharmony.

Illness of any kind must surely be based on this dynamic, unless it is environmentally generated. And the path to health is certainly in the direction of generating a base frequency in the chakras and bringing the chakras into entrainment one with the other so that there exists a primary frequency, a harmony, and ultimately a full symphony of beautiful chakratic music throughout one's energy system and cellular presence. Then and only then can one have health and peace, let alone clear thoughts, radiant emotions, and spiritual realization.

I personally use the humming meditation I just taught you regularly to generate a primary resonance in my body. Then, once I have established the deep, pervading resonance of the hum throughout my being, I am ready to enjoy chanting the specific sounds for each chakra.

At this point in our exploration of kundalini awakening, I offer you this primal entrainment meditation of humming and hope you devote regular time to its powers. You can do this humming meditation anywhere, anytime, since it is an inner sound, not vocalized to the outside world. I do hope that I have made my point, and that you hum your way through life from here on out!

## THE FIFTH-CHAKRA CHANT

You will notice that the humming meditation is actually nothing more nor less than the last third of every chakra chant. The fifth-chakra mantra is, for instance, *HAM* or *HANG*. Of course for a closed-lip humming sound, *HANG* doesn't work, so we turn to *HAM* for this perfect parallel to the *Mmmmm* sound.

It is the first consonant of each mantra that differentiates it from the mantras of the other chakras. There are deep and often conflicting traditions regarding the powers of the different letters of the

Sanskrit alphabet. For instance, you have noticed an increasing number of petals around each mandala as we have progressed up the chakras. In ancient Yogic teachings, the petals are associated with different letters in the Sanskrit alphabet, communicating various symbolic meanings for each mandala. The fifth-chakra mandala has all sixteen of the vowels of the Sanskrit alphabet, each vowel on a different petal.

The analysis and interpretation of the meanings of each of the Sanskrit vowels could fill a book, and does not in my opinion offer a great deal of pragmatic help in the challenge of direct meditational expansion of consciousness. It is a very cerebral, fifth-chakra mental exercise, especially for those of us from Western culture, where the Sanskrit alphabet has no meaning at all.

What is of value is knowing that each of the consonants beginning the mantra for each chakra has a meaning, and it is a clear meaning. The *L* that begins the Root Chakra mantra stands for the earth element, and pulls the consciousness down to the base of the spine. The *V* that begins the mantra for the Sexual Chakra is related to water, the second element. The *R* that begins the Power Chakra stands for fire, the element of that third chakra. The *Y* beginning the Heart Chakra stands for air, the element of the fourth chakra. And as you can guess, the *H* that begins the mantra for the fifth chakra represents space, or ether.

The more you chant these mantras, the more you will feel an actual pulling of your attention to the chakra that is associated with the consonant that begins the mantra. This sometimes seems like magic, although I'm certain it is simply the acting out of a basic law that science has not yet identified.

Take time now to explore the fifth-chakra chant . . . put the book down after reading this paragraph, so you can tune in to your breathing . . . expand your consciousness

to include your whole body here in the present moment
. . . close your eyes perhaps . . . hum a bit to yourself to
set all your chakras vibrating . . . and begin to allow the
fifth-chakra mantra, *HAM* or *HANG*, to come alive
deep inside you—and manifest. . . .

## THE COMMUNICATION MANDALA

As we progress through the chakras from bottom to top, we
find the colors becoming cooler and cooler, and the vibrations of the
colors faster and shorter. The earth frequencies are the longest and
lowest, as we would expect. As we rise up into the heavens, the
frequencies quicken, and the colors move from the red of the earth to
the blue of the heavens.

Zachary has depicted the fifth chakra in accordance with the
ancient texts, in a transformational presentation that mixes the green
from the Heart Chakra below with the deep blue from the sixth
chakra above, rather than doing the whole mandala in medium blue,
as it would be rendered if the fifth chakra were static.

Thus the effect of this mandala is exactly what our contemporary minds really need—it serves to spread our yang, masculine fifth-
chakra awareness out broadly enough so that it comes immediately
into communion with the yin, feminine energies of the fourth and sixth
chakras that bound it.

When you look directly to the center of the throat mandala, you
will find that the alternating green and deep-blue colors of the sixteen
petals begin to merge into one medium-blue. Thus the fifth-chakra
color does suddenly appear. Such is the visual magic that Zachary
has offered us.

As I have mentioned before, each chakra is associated with an
animal. These animals often appear spontaneously when you are
looking at a mandala. In this case, very often people see the elephant

of the first chakra reappearing, only this time as a great white beast. Sometimes the animal that appears for this chakra is a white bull, sometimes a white lion.

Animals do possess certain primal qualities, basic vibratory energies that we can make contact with, "entrain with," to use the scientific terminology. I do not suggest overtly forcing the image of an animal into your mind while meditating. But please do be open to the appearance of an animal right in the middle of the mandala.

Likewise, and this should be stated especially for this fifth chakra so strongly associated with visions, when you are looking into the central white space of each mandala, you should be open to any sort of vision appearing before your eyes. Again, I am not of the school that actively conjures up images to meditate upon. In this regard I am more a Zen Buddhist than a Hindu. My feeling is that we should do our best to move beyond visions, since they are always influenced by our personal fantasies and unconscious activities.

But when they do come, this is perfectly fine. Experience them, enjoy them—but don't become fixated on them. The world of Maya—of illusion, of holding on to images and visions instead of moving beyond them—is a fifth-chakra function. Always be ready to let go of your visions in order to move up into sixth-chakra, nonconceptual consciousness. Thus this fifth-chakra mandala points toward the deep blue of the sixth, intuitive chakra and down to the green of the fourth-chakra heart center. Be open to vast fifth-chakra visions that play out your mind's conceptual imagery of spiritual awakening, and be ready to let go and move on at any moment.

A definite safety valve that will keep you from getting lost in fifth-chakra visions and astral experiences is to stay aware of your breathing throughout—this will ground you. Remember the Breath-Anchor meditation (page 41) I taught you early in the book. It is an essential meditation to take along with you in your explorations of the deeper realms of fifth-chakra experience.

And so, enough words about this chakra. You know where it lies in the middle of your humming sensation in your throat.

Breathe and let the vibration of the hum awaken this chakra. Chant *HAM* or *HANG* and further activate the fifth chakra.

Turn to the mandala and ride the fourth vehicle. . . .

# 10

# Merging Mind with Spirit
# (Sixth Chakra)

*The first five chakras* have been located down below the mind itself. Now, with the sixth chakra, we reach the point where we are consciously focusing on the part of our body that in fact is doing the conscious focusing: the mind is finally looking directly at itself.

Whereas the fifth chakra was the chakra of sound, of relatively slow vibrations passing through the medium of air molecules in our planetary atmosphere, the sixth chakra is the chakra of light, of vibratory energy traveling remarkably fast, not needing an atmospheric medium for its transmission.

Sound is an earthly phenomenon, created by friction of molecules one against the other. Light is an intergalactic phenomenon created by radiative emissions from atomic and molecular systems. We earthly beings can create sound through our gross physiological functioning, by propelling air out of our lungs and setting this air vibrating with our taut vocal cords. But we can not create light in such a mechanical way. Light lies beyond our personal powers of creation.

Our primary source of light comes, of course, from our own sun burning brightly through the aeons. Even our coal and oil deposits that provide nighttime light when transformed into electricity come

from solar sources. Hydroelectric generators also have as their ultimate energy source the solar-caused weather patterns of the earth.
Only nuclear reactors create their own light and energy, and this is
through mimicking the sun's nuclear furnaces. So when we reflect
upon the sixth chakra, we are reflecting upon our relationship with
the center of our solar system—the sun itself.

The sixth chakra is located between our two eyes and a little up.
Our eyes are, of course, our main sensory means for receiving light
into our bodies and transforming the information carried by reflected
light into visual images that give us our impressions of the outside
world.

It is very easy to get lost in intellectual speculations about this
mysterious sixth chakra. Teachers such as Thakin Kung, however,
strongly suggest that we not indulge in thinking overmuch about the
sixth chakra—otherwise we cloud our direct perception of this energy center, and in a very real way avoid rising up from fifth-chakra
thinking to experience it intimately.

Many people remain chronically down in the fifth, conceptual
chakra, thinking grandiose thoughts about the sixth chakra, but
avoiding a direct encounter with it. Making the break with the fifth
chakra proves immensely difficult for many people, as I have found
out both with myself and with clients and students over the years.
How we cling to our concepts! But ultimately, the sixth chakra is
beyond concepts.

So—let me give you just a few key inputs at the conceptual
level, to provide a springboard for moving beyond concepts into the
realm of sixth-chakra awakening. Then we will focus on the actual
meditative techniques for making this move.

At this point in our discussion, we need to reflect on a primal
chakratic concept that has existed for several thousand years. According to Hindu and Buddhist understandings of the intricate
workings of the kundalini energy system, there are two major conduits through which kundalini energy rises up the spine. These

conduits are named Ida and Pingala. Respectively they channel the yin and the yang flows of kundalini energy up the body.

These female and male opposites intertwine intimately like lovers as they twist their way up through the first five chakras. Then something quite remarkable happens in the sixth—they merge!

According to the Sanskrit tradition, they merge in the pineal gland, or perhaps—as some contemporary neurologists suggest—in the pituitary. Here they generate what is called the Third Eye that lies within the brain, just behind the center of the brow. And it is here—where the earthly opposites unite, where yin and yang become one, where the unmanifest and the manifest are joined in spiritual marriage—that we find the sixth chakra.

When I was a boy I remember reading over and over again in the Gospel of Matthew the following statement attributed to Jesus: "If therefore thine eye be single, thy whole body shall be filled with light." What in the world could he have meant by that? I pondered. Later at seminary I attempted to get deeper into the mystery of those words, but found little guidance in the Protestant tradition.

The real answer, at least for me, came through my parallel studies of the Yogic tradition, which very clearly explained that when a human being finally lets go of concepts, of dualities—which is to say, when the Ida and the Pingala merge—a great flood of light comes into the body caused by the awakening of the *bija* energy of the sixth chakra.

As a boy I often experienced temporary awakenings of the sixth chakra, where my body would suddenly be filled with light and I would lose normal consciousness for a short time—overwhelmed by the ecstatic experience of merging with the universe, of moving beyond dualities and into the pure white light.

When I would try to talk with anyone except my grandmother about these experiences, I would be laughed at, or simply not taken seriously. For a time I thought perhaps I was crazy, and I did my best not to allow such mystic interludes to overwhelm me.

But as a young man, I found myself interested in all the religious explanations of white-light experiences. And in meditation I found I was able to consciously encourage this experience. Furthermore, I found the Yogic descriptions of sixth-chakra visions to be almost exactly the same as my personal experiences. It was such a relief to find out that I wasn't the only person who had such momentary lapses from normal consciousness.

However, I made the youthful mistake of fixating on this chakra, and as a result for several years the health of my overall energy system was quite off balance. I was aiming to remain in light all the time, to forever leave darkness behind. I wanted my spiritual lights to be on every moment.

What I was actually doing was denying the more universal reality that in order for there to be light, there must also be darkness; for there to be yang there must also be yin; for there to be Ida there must also be Pingala. Spiritual maturity requires a willingness to welcome both of the opposite polarities into the whole picture of spiritual reality—and to then move beyond dualism altogether. This is the sixth-chakra experience.

As you approach your own sixth chakra in this program, I encourage you to venture into light, but also embrace darkness. Expand your concept of spiritual realization to include both extremes, and find your center in the middle. Rise up into the bright light of the sixth and ultimately the seventh chakra and also plunge regularly into the depths of your primordial darkness, the black hole of your first chakra that rises up from the center of the Earth.

In a very real sense the human experience of duality—of darkness and light—comes from our polar relationship with the Earth and the sun. It is the energetic relationship between these two force fields that makes life possible. And it is from embracing both the darkness of the center of the Earth and the infinite brightness of the center of the sun that we are able to enter into the sixth chakra, where the two eyes become one, where darkness and light merge as a unity.

What do you get when you mix equal parts of infinite bright light with infinite darkness?

Answer: a balanced sixth-chakra experience.

## LET YOUR LITTLE LIGHT SHINE

In my childhood, with my father playing a raucous honky-tonk piano, we often sang a song that included the following line: "This little light of mine, I'm going to let it shine. . . ."

This is a beautiful sixth-chakra mantra in itself.

We do become radiant beings when we begin to channel sixth-chakra light into our entire energy system. However, the challenge of channeling light into the world through our sixth chakra is not the whole story at this point. The equal challenge is to learn how to bring this light down step-by-step into each of the lower chakras, to empower them with spiritual energy from above.

I hope you understand by now how each chakra, beginning with the Root Chakra, serves to help us to expand and activate the next higher chakra. At the same time, the fulfillment of the higher chakras lies also in allowing a downward movement of the higher-chakra energies into the lower chakras, so that true equality is gained in the energetic system. The Old Testament tells us that God created both the darkness and the light, as equals. Circulating the light into the darkness is as important as turning the darkness into light.

The beautiful thing about the sixth chakra is that, as I pointed out already, we finally experience darkness and light merging, so that as spiritual beings we transcend all prejudice regarding light and darkness, regarding higher and lower chakras, regarding heaven and Earth. As the Buddha was quoted saying in the beginning of this book: true enlightenment means letting go of even the concept of Enlightenment itself.

Thus as soon as you attain sixth-chakra awakening of any intensity at all, your spiritual challenge is to expand so that this light floods equally throughout the chakra system. If you just remain fixated on the sixth chakra, indulging in the light, you throw your entire spiritual presence seriously off center. I know that many spiritual teachers disagree with me on this point, and I certainly give you the freedom to disagree with me too, and to fixate primarily on the higher chakras if you find this your true path. I am simply communicating my experience.

Before we go further, I want to give you time to reflect on your own experiences with sixth-chakra light. Pause a few moments, breathe, expand your awareness to include your whole body here in the present moment, and let yourself look back over your own life, to remember times when you felt very bright, full of energy and light, mystically atuned with God and nature, with your sixth chakra radiating light. . . .

## The Magic of the *Kumbhaka* Breath

I have already taught you one breath meditation that is very effective for bringing the kundalini energy up to awaken the sixth chakra, as it does also for the other chakras—the alternate-nostril breathing technique where, in order to bring consciousness and energy up the spine, you breathe through one nostril, then with a finger or thumb close that nostril, and switch to breathe through the other nostril, then switch back and continue with this pattern.

I now want to teach you another basic *pranayama* technique for awakening the chakras. This is a practice called *kumbhaka* breath control. There are two opposite states of *kumbhaka*. One is when your breath is held after full inhalation (the lungs being completely full of air), the other when your breath is held after full exhalation (the lungs being emptied of all air).

When you inhale and then hold your breath, you very directly pull kundalini energy up the spine from your depths and hold this energy at the top of your energetic system. Then when you exhale and hold your breath at the bottom of your exhale, you pull light and energy from the top chakras down to the lower ones. In this way, with each inhale, you actively bring kundalini energy upwards to awaken the higher chakras, and also to encourage the inflow of light from above. Then on each exhale you bring this light down to your depths. Thus you gain the perfect mixing of heaven and earth, and the balancing of your energetic system at higher and higher levels of consciousness.

Let me present you with a clear, simple, safe program for employing *kumbhaka* breath retention while meditating upon the chakras, and especially for awakening the sixth chakra. You will want to devote considerable time over the years to mastering this seemingly simple pattern of breathing if you want to fully tap into its power. It is without question extremely powerful, and deeply rewarding.

### *Kumbhaka One: The Balanced Breath*

Here is perhaps the most important of all the *pranayama* breathing meditations. Of the three different techniques I am going to teach you now, I suggest that you use this Kumbhaka One breathing pattern most often—to awaken your entire chakra system at once in a balanced charging experience:

*Inhale* (through both nostrils) for the count of TWO. . . .
*Hold* at the top for the count of FOUR. . . .
*Exhale* for the count of SIX. . . .
*Hold* at the bottom for the count of FOUR. . . .
And *repeat* this cycle. . . .

You will find that this particular breathing pattern almost always awakens kundalini energy in your system and encourages this energy to rise up your spine. The rapid inhale to the count of two, where you must fill your lungs quickly, serves especially to charge your body and pull energy all the way up the spine.

The breath held for four counts at the top of your inhale serves to hold your consciousness in the sixth and seventh chakras, so a flooding of light can come into your body from above and mix with the upflow of kundalini energy.

The slow exhale to the count of six gently encourages the energy and light to come floating down through your chakras, often as a blissful shower of white light. Be sure to exhale completely so that you bring your consciousness all the way down to the Root Chakra.

As you hold for four counts on empty, you again tap into the kundalini energy from below so that you are ready to bring this energy up the spine with your next rapid inhale.

The ultimate effect of this breathing pattern will be to bring your attention to the central point, the Heart Chakra, while also charging and balancing the peripheral chakras at the same time. Try this for yourself now for six to twelve breath cycles, and notice how your kundalini experience is enhanced even if this is your very first experience with *kumbhaka* breathing. . . .

## *Kumbhaka Two: Super-Charging Upward*

This second *pranayama* breathing pattern is to be done with a bit of caution (moderately) when you want to quickly bring a great deal of kundalini energy up the spine to awaken higher levels of activity in the top two chakras.

The pattern here is to inhale slowly and deeply to the count of six . . . hold for a count of six . . . then exhale for a count of four . . . then with no held breath at all at the bottom, inhale again slowly to the count of six . . . hold for six . . . exhale for the count of four . . . then without holding the breath at the bottom, inhale again for the count of six . . . and continue with this pattern for the amount of time you consider prudent. I will write the pattern out in simple format:

*Inhale* for the count of SIX. . . .
*Hold* for the count of SIX. . . .
*Exhale* for the count of FOUR. . . .
Don't hold your breath at all at the bottom.
And *repeat* the pattern a number of times. . . .

This breathing formula focuses most of your attention up high in your body and chakras, continually bringing kundalini energy up the spine to the higher energy centers. While you hold your breath at the top of your inhales, your focus goes naturally to your sixth-chakra, third-eye location. Then you simply let the air fall out of you on the exhale. This usually happens in a four-count period of time. You should always feel free to vary the count slightly if you find your breathing requesting more or less time on one of the phases. I am giving you a general formula. You can adapt it as time goes by to your particular energetic personality.

By not holding your breath at all at the bottom of the exhale, you actively maintain your attention in the higher chakras. This breathing pattern is an ultimate breath pump—a kundalini energy pump—with remarkable effects on consciousness. Try it for yourself and experience its magic in your own chakra system. . . .

### Kumbhaka Three: Calming the Energetic System

Very often, as a breathing antidote to other kundalini meditations, you will want to employ a calming meditation that will smooth out your energies and bring you down deep into your lower chakras again. Kumbhaka Three is that meditation. You should use it regularly to make sure you don't overactivate your kundalini experience.

This is just the reverse of the Kumbhaka Two breath pattern. You exhale for the count of six . . . then hold your breath for the count of six . . . then inhale to the count of four . . . and without holding your breath at the top at all, exhale again to the count of six . . . and continue with this pattern for as long as you want. Again, let me write that in brief outline form:

> *Exhale* for the count of SIX. . . .
> *Hold* for the count of SIX. . . .
> *Inhale* for the count of FOUR. . . .
> Don't hold your breath at all at the top.
> And *repeat* the pattern a number of times. . . .

With this breath meditation you move your mind's attention down deep into your lower chakras, down into the solidness of the Earth under you, while you avoid focusing on the top chakras. The effects of this meditation pattern were studied by a research team I was working with at the New Jersey Neuropsychiatric Institute. We found that while doing this breathing pattern a person's heartbeat would quickly slow down, blood pressure would go down dramatically, and a general calming of the emotions and mind would result.

I have been teaching this pattern ever since to nervous clients and to students who tend to overindulge in kundalini stimulation. I heartily recommend it to you as well. You can do it anytime, anywhere, when you want to consciously calm yourself and ground your energetic system down into the Earth. Experiment with this pattern right now if you want to, and begin to tap into its powers for generating relaxation and inner balance. . . .

## AWAKENING THE MAGIC *OM*

Finally, after all our chakratic adventures, we now arrive at the fountain of that famous chant *OM*, or *AOUM* as it is sometimes expressed. You will notice immediately that this sound is lacking the usual masculine consonant at the beginning of the mantra. As would be said in Hindu teachings, we have now left the concrete, manifest consonants behind, and moved into a spirit realm of nonmaterial vowel sounds.

The sixth chakra is most definitely a feminine chakra, teamed up with the Sexual Chakra and the Heart Chakra to create a super-triad of yin energies in the body, each surrounded by masculine energy centers. As you probably know, in popular psychology we associate our logical, thinking, problem-solving mind (the fifth chakra) with masculine qualities, and our intuitive, spiritual, artistic mind (the sixth chakra) with feminine qualities. In this regard modern feelings about these qualities are identical to the ancient teachings.

Let me present the seven chakras from a slightly different perspective than usual to encourage new insight into the feminine-masculine interplays in your energy system as a whole. Instead of visualizing the chakras running up and down, let's lay the feminine-masculine, yin-yang chakra configuration onto a horizontal plane, so you can gain a new mental vision of these relationships:

| Root-1 | Sex-2 | Will-3 | Heart-4 | Sound-5 | Light-6 | Crown-7 |
|--------|--------|--------|---------|---------|---------|---------|
| MALE | FEMALE | MALE | FEMALE | MALE | FEMALE | MALE |
| Yang | + | Yang | + | Yang | + | Yang |
| | Yin | + | Yin | + | Yin | |

*

This is the Chinese way of viewing the balance of yin and yang in the human energetic system. The strong masculine chakras are on the outside extremes of the energy system, encountering the raw light and energy coming from above and below. This energy is then transformed as it passes into the female chakras of Sex and Light, which are an integral pair. Then this refined energy and light moves into the interior masculine chakras of Will and Sound (Communication), another integral pair. And finally the energy reaches the center-point of the energetic system, where it is transmuted into the ultimate power of the heart—love.

The three feminine mantras of the chakra system are, as you now know, *VAM, YAM,* and *AOUM.* The *VAM* sound is a very strong, sexual energy. The *YAM* sound is much softer, more balanced in the heart. And the *OM* or *AOUM* sound is pure, soft—yet penetrating to the very depths and heights of the universe.

Each of these sounds wakes up not only the chakra for which it is directly associated, but the other two feminine chakras as well. And as these chakras are woken up by sound vibration, they naturally stimulate the male chakras beside them. This is how chakra balancing happens—the interplay of all the chakras serves to spread the energy evenly throughout the system, unless one is blocked in certain chakras, or doing kundalini meditations that specifically push the energy in only one direction.

Very often in Hindu meditational practice, students are assigned the *OM* chant as the primary mantra. *OM* has become somewhat of a spiritual cliché in our own society, because a number of meditation teachers have taught this mantra as the one key to enlightenment—if you sit and chant it over and over again ad infinitum.

Under an excellent teacher, this single-minded approach often works. The Zen tradition, for instance, often has students chant just one sound for years: *MU.* If a student is disciplined enough, and already well-balanced emotionally and cognitively, this type of meditation will suffice.

But for most of us, with quite confused and imbalanced chakras when we start our meditations, more is recommended than just chanting *OM* or *MU* for an hour a day until something stupendous happens. At the same time, although *OM* might not be the total answer to spiritual development, it is a great pleasure to explore the

*OM* meditation here where it is properly located, as the primary sixth-chakra chant. This mantra does deserve a great deal of attention in our spiritual lives. It can be a pathway into the great white light and beyond, and of course back again as well.

Let me give you full opportunity to begin to awaken the magical powers of *OM* or *AOUM*. First let the *AOUM* sound manifest deep within you. . . . Now let it become a vocal sound. . . . Let the sound vibrate within and around you. . . . As you chant, allow your attention to tune in to the Third Eye in the middle of your forehead. . . . Be open to an experience you have never had before. . . .

## THE SIXTH-CHAKRA MANDALA

We now come to the visual impression of the sixth chakra. Here we return to absolute simplicity, as Zachary has aptly portrayed it. The basic image is of the Ida and Pingala energy upflows merging in the center of white light.

In a very important sense, this mandala represents the two sides of the human brain, the two opposite extremes of cognitive and intuitive. As always, Zachary is pointing in his mandalas toward the movement into the next chakra—in this case the seventh chakra, where both intuitive and cognitive functions of the mind fall away, and we merge with the Godhead beyond our mind. Thus Zachary points us upward with this vision of the opposites on the extremes, and the pure white light in the middle.

However, the color energies in this mandala move us also in the opposite direction, down into the color of the cognitive fifth-chakra center, so that we have a direct map in the other direction, helping us to remember that the aim is not just up and up and up. The aim is a flow in both directions.

The animal for the sixth chakra is quite perfectly the owl, who sometimes stares back at us from this yantra. The question of the owl is a mantra in itself: "Hoo, hoo . . . who are you?" Taken as a Zen *koan*, as a question that leads to spiritual realization, the owl's chant is certainly to be oft reflected upon. . . .

The time has come again to turn to the insert, find the mandala for the sixth chakra, and experience for yourself your present inner spiritual reality. Meditation is always a looking to see what is happening in the present moment deep within—and then a charging of this reality with heightened spiritual energy to bring about transformation. So calmly go through either a full kundalini meditation now, or experiment with just the sixth-chakra vehicles, as you open yourself to the visual element of this chakra. . . .

# 11

# Infinite Bliss
# (Seventh Chakra)

*All three of my* main kundalini teachers refused categorically to discuss the seventh chakra. They felt that this chakra should be encountered without preconceptions of any kind to interfere with direct experience.

It is therefore with a bit of hesitation that I write anything at all about this ultimate chakra. Still, because I am not working with you personally, face to face, I do feel it best to provide you with a minimal conceptual vision of the nature of the seventh chakra.

The Sanskrit name of this energy center is *sahasrara*, which means "to multiply by a thousand." In a looser translation, *sahasrara* means tapping into the infinite spiritual dimensions that lie beyond the personal parameters of consciousness. Awakening the seventh chakra is most definitely an experience in which we transcend our individual minds and enter into perfect conscious harmony with the infinite spiritual wholeness of the universe.

The ancient Chinese book of wisdom, the *Tao Te Ching* by Lao-tzu, begins by saying that it is impossible to vocalize a name for the ultimate God. In like manner there is no chant for this chakra. The sound that comes to you in meditation upon this chakra is nothing less than the sound of the universe vibrating directly within you.

Sometimes in Western culture, the awakening of the seventh chakra is called "receiving Christ consciousness." But even this label tends to stand between a person and seventh-chakra experience. Christ Consciousness is a transcendent concept, but still it is a concept, which ultimately must be put aside—as we have already seen—in order to move into both sixth and seventh-chakra awakening.

Let me simply say that the seventh chakra is the swirling energy vortex located right in the top of your head and swirling also above the top of your head, where you transcend individual consciousness and tap into infinite consciousness. You cease to exist as a separate entity when you are in seventh-chakra consciousness. "You" are gone. There is no "you." There is only infinite consciousness, of which you are an integral part.

This egoless experience brings you into an ultimate state of spiritual bliss. In fact, the remarkable thing about seventh-chakra consciousness is that it seems to be bliss itself. The universal consciousness, if we were to give it any label at all, would be Bliss Consciousness. This is all we can say.

## EFFORTLESS ATTAINMENT

This bliss state is not something we can force into existence in our minds. It comes only after we have prepared ourselves through such techniques as we have been learning in this book. Even then, it comes of itself, in its own good time.

Sometimes we move into seventh-chakra bliss after doing formal kundalini meditation for a half hour to an hour. Sometimes it also comes to us spontaneously, when we least expect it. I suspect that each and every one of us has slipped into seventh-chakra bliss many times in our lives, especially as children when we knew this bliss state as the permeating reality, the underlying feeling of being alive. It is the Garden of Eden that we inhabited as children—when everything in our environment and emotional charge was auspicious for such communion with the divine.

As adults, right after lovemaking we often momentarily slip into this seventh-chakra bliss state. And sometimes we can simply walk outside on an autumn morning, take one whiff of the air, feel the breeze on our cheeks, and lapse into bliss.

The often quoted cowboy saying from my own childhood sums it up perfectly: "You can lead a horse to water but you can't make it drink." You can move the kundalini energy up the spine dutifully through the lower chakras, but when you come to the highest energy vortex, you cannot make your soul drink of the infinite nectar of the seventh chakra. You can bring yourself to the doorway through breathing, focusing, chanting, and meditating on the mandalas—but your actual passage into the bliss state, into the infinite grace of spiritual union with the divine, comes and goes completely of itself, effortlessly.

## BLISS BREATHING

As you turn your attention, in your daily meditations, from the sixth chakra to the seventh, your breathing should become totally uncontrolled, spontaneous, calm, as if the universe is "breathing you" while you make no effort at all.

This is one of the qualities of the seventh-chakra experience—that your breathing takes on a completely different feeling in your chest. Bliss is definitely a breathing experience. It is the feeling of pure joy at being alive—participating in the great breathing experience of all life on this planet.

I say no more, except to encourage you in each kundalini meditation to be open to this blissful breathing experience. . . .

## SEVENTH-CHAKRA FOCUSING

You have almost surely already noticed that when you turn your attention to one chakra, your mind has the ability to expand and be aware of another chakra at the same time. This happens most readily with chakras that are next to each other, or with chakras that are of the same yin-yin or yang-yang valence.

Therefore, when you turn your attention to the first chakra, your attention readily expands to include the first and second chakra together. This is the natural beauty of kundalini meditation. And often when you focus on the second chakra, you will often find the fourth chakra entering your consciousness at a harmonious higher resonance with the second chakra.

The ultimate aim, as I am sure you realize by now, is to expand your consciousness so that you are aware of all the chakras at once. This can happen almost simultaneously after you become practiced in mental expansion.

Especially when you do the full half-hour kundalini meditation I will describe soon—moving your attention step-by-step up the chakra centers and doing the meditations for each chakra in turn— you will find that by the time you reach the seventh chakra, you have already made intimate contact with this chakra many times in the meditation. So arriving at the top chakra is simply a final expansion into pure bliss, with all the other chakras resonating below the seventh chakra in a veritable chakratic symphony of immense power and beauty.

## SEVENTH-CHAKRA SILENT MANTRA

As you shift from sixth-chakra chanting of the *OM* to the seventh chakra, simply allow the *AOUM* chant to fall silent. This vibratory energy will continue throughout your chakra system. Often it is the path that you find yourself following up into the seventh chakra. It becomes a silent but all-pervasive mantra. It is the sound of the universe singing, waking up the feeling of bliss in every cell in your body.

Right when you feel yourself entering the bliss state, be sure that you remain aware of your breathing, so that it doesn't contract at the vastness of the experience. Be aware—but don't control. After all there can be no control in paradise. All your discipline must be put aside and left behind. You are becoming a creature who is perfectly entrained, in harmony with and resonating in spontaneous joyful abandon with the universe. Perfect control turns into its equal and opposite at this point—spontaneous participation.

Alan Watts sometimes spoke of seventh-chakra bliss as an encounter with the Great Guffaw—the universal laughter that permeates all of life. Gurdjieff spoke in similar terms several times in his writings. There is a laughter that is not vocalized when in the bliss state—but it is there, tickling every cell, vibrating with the pure pleasure of being.

My recommendation is that with every kundalini meditation you do, even if it is for five minutes as I will describe in the following chapter, you move your attention up to the seventh chakra—not expecting a vast blissful encounter with the divine every time, but regularly looking in this direction so that you become intimate friends with the infinite.

The key thing is not to relate to the seventh chakra as a scary state of consciousness. Wilhelm Reich was quoted as saying that the seventh chakra is just the place where you hang your hat. It is you. You are it. Don't let people scare you about encountering yourself, even if that self is infinite expansion!

## THE SEVENTH MANDALA

The mandala that Zachary has drawn for the seventh chakra is a vision of paradise. It will serve to guide you deeper in the general direction of bliss. It is the vision of a crown with sixteen radiating petals. These sixteen outer petals of the Crown Chakra are perfectly formed so as to represent the gathering of light and energy from all directions around the crown of your head.

Keep in mind that, as kundalini energy rises up into the seventh chakra, it bursts free of your personal energy system and merges with the infinite energy system beyond you. At the same time, unless you have seriously unbalanced your chakras, a remarkable sense of light and energy will flow into your body, filling each chakra with bliss, and healing personal imbalances with the universal power of love.

Love and bliss: these two words are perhaps inseparable. It is said in many of the sacred writings that one cannot attain seventh-chakra realization unless the fourth chakra is radiant with universal love. There is a very definite marriage of love and bliss when the seventh chakra comes awake. Not only does light flow into the body, but infinite love as well. They are, in this state, one and the same.

By the time you have drawn kundalini energy up through all six chakras, this energy, beginning as raw sexual energy, has become transformed into will, compassion, knowledge, and wisdom. And each time the energy has risen up through a chakra, this chakra has also experienced an equal downflowing of light and love from above.

So in your daily meditations, even before you turn your attention to the seventh chakra, you will have experienced a beautiful down-pouring of blissful, loving energy through your Crown Chakra. But only when you turn your conscious attention to the seventh chakra itself do you directly experience this radiant energy at its source.

No one knows what this "energy" really is, as I mentioned earlier. I use the word "energy" for lack of a better one in our language. Light is of course a form of energy. The Holy Spirit is energy. Love is energy. The electromagnetic force field of our own body is energy. So is the thousandfold force field of the planet we live upon. There also exist manifestations of energy in the universe that we

can experience directly but cannot conceptually or physically manipulate or understand. Meditation is the tool for gaining access to this
high-level energy. The first and the seventh chakras are the points
where subtle flows of this energy enter our chakratic system. The
heart is where these energies unite.

When you look at Zachary's seventh-chakra mandala, you will
see that the petals are both "transmitters" of kundalini energy into the
universal consciousness and at the same time "receivers" of universal
energy into your personal body. This is how it should be. Two into
one.

Some scientists have reduced seventh-chakra experiences to a
sudden hyperactivation of the pineal or pituitary gland in the brain.
Certainly this could explain many of the blissful states we enter into
when we merge with the Universal Consciousness. Biochemistry is
part of the infinite dance of the universe as it manifests in our bodies
and minds.

But the experience itself is an affirmation that there is more to
life than deductive scientific reasoning, and there is more to kundalini
awakening than biochemistry, the biochemical dimension being but
one finite way of viewing infinity.

Without further words, turn to the seventh-chakra mandala and
explore your own deepening awareness of the divine. . . .

# 12

# Love as
# the Kundalini Center

*You now have a* solid grounding in all the seven chakras of your body's energetic system. If you take time regularly to do the meditations I have described, you can advance deeper and more consciously into kundalini pleasure, power, compassion, wisdom, and realization.

But for most people it is usually not enough just to know the basic kundalini meditations as a general spiritual discipline. What is needed for most people, to succeed in making this program a lifetime spiritual path, is a concrete assortment of meditational plans, which you can choose from depending on your present mood, energy level, time available for meditating, and meditational environment.

In this chapter I first want to teach you a very short "seven-breath" chakra-integration meditation that can be done in just a minute or two. With this meditation in hand, there is actually always time to do your kundalini meditations! And often, five such short meditations in the midst of everyday life can be just as significant as a single half-hour or hour meditation done once a day in retreat. The need for regular discipline continues to exist in contemporary society, for finding time to be alone to meditate for at least half an hour a day. But there are many shorter times each day for brief kundalini meditation, and we should regularly take advantage of such times.

# The Seven-Breath Meditation

Just pause for one to two minutes . . . tune in to your breathing experience for a few breaths . . . expand to include your heartbeat and whole body here in the present moment . . . see what energy flows are happening spontaneously in your nervous system. . . .

(1) On your next breath (the first breath of the formal meditation) chant *LAM* or *LANG* as you exhale, either silently or out loud depending on your situation . . . constrict the sphincter muscle and abdomen muscles to move your attention instantly to the first chakra . . . as you inhale, allow a beautiful upflow of kundalini energy to begin to rise up through your body . . . and if your visualization ability is sharp, let the first-chakra mandala come into your mind as well. . . .

(2) As you begin your second exhale, shift your attention to your genitals . . . set your chakras vibrating beautifully with the sexual-chakra chant of *VAM* or *VANG* until you are completely empty of air . . . remain empty a moment as you open yourself to an inflow of kundalini energy higher into your energy system . . . feel the energy flowing down into you from above at the same time . . . and as you inhale, let the energy flows increase . . . and perhaps visualize the Sexual-Chakra mandala as well while you slowly inhale. . . .

(3) Hold your breath at the top of your inhale a moment, so that you again experience your entire energy system as a whole . . . now let your third exhale begin, moving your attention up into your Power Chakra . . . chant silently or aloud the third-chakra mantra of *RAM* or *RANG* . . . constrict sphincter muscle and abdomen muscles again as you exhale completely . . .

hold on empty while you feel the vibrations continuing in your system . . . inhale and let the power mandala come into your mind . . . be open to the inflow of light and energy from above and below. . . .

(4) Hold on full breath a moment . . . and now exhale slowly while chanting the fourth-chakra *YAM* or *YANG*, focus on the Heart Chakra . . . raise your arms out to the sides if you want this physical focusing on the Heart Chakra . . . hold on empty while energy flows through your entire chakra system . . . and visualize the fourth-chakra mandala as you inhale slowly. . . .

(5) Hold at the top of your inhale . . . let your awareness rise up into your throat . . . slowly exhale while you chant the fifth-chakra *HAM* or *HANG* . . . hold on empty and feel your chakras from top to bottom . . . visualize the fifth-chakra mandala while you slowly inhale . . . bring energy up higher and higher. . . .

(6) Now hold again at the top, and let your awareness shift up to the Third Eye between your brows . . . exhale while the chant *OM* vibrates through your entire spiritual being . . . hold on empty to bring the higher energies and light down deep into your lower chakras . . . and as you inhale, visualize the sixth-chakra mandala as you let kundalini energy come rushing through your energy system. . . .

(7) Hold a long time at the top of your inhale, as you shift your consciousness up to the top of your head, to the Crown Chakra, the union of your personal presence with the infinite presence . . . be filled with light from above . . . and now exhale slowly, allowing a beautiful flood of light and love to come into your body from top to bottom . . . become empty . . . let your spiritual consciousness expand infinitely at the same time. . . .

## THE SEVEN-BREATH MEDITATION

Once this Seven-Breath meditation becomes ingrained into your everyday routines as a spiritual habit, you will find that you can go very deeply into kundalini awakening in a very short period of time. In this hectic world, such an approach to meditation is vital, even though traditional meditation teachers would frown at the brevity of the session. As I said before, one breath during which you are conscious of your breathing is worth a thousand breaths without such consciousness.

The Seven-Breath meditation is simple—a synthesis of the entire chakra program you have learned in this book. Remember that you can do the meditation either standing, sitting, or lying down, while driving a car, working at your desk, digging a ditch, eating a meal, lying in bed, waiting for a dental appointment, sitting at a board meeting. . . .

Following this Seven-Breath, seven-chakra meditation, breathe quietly in a spontaneous manner for as long as you like or have time for, so that you live consciously within the heightened energetic reality of your spiritual system.

Then off you go with this increased spiritual charge, to do whatever you are in position to do next, spreading pure white light and radiant love in whatever you do—teaching by the example of your own energetic system, and letting other people get a contact-high from your expansive spiritual presence. . . .

## THE SIMULTANEOUS MEDITATION EXPERIENCE

As I have mentioned briefly before, and as you will discover for yourself as you progress with your daily meditations, you possess an amazing capability to learn to do a meditation that involves several steps, then to merge the steps into a simultaneous happening. Much of the magic of the program I have presented involves this potential of human consciousness to instantaneously become aware of the entire chakra system at once. This is our aim. Everything in every meditation technique moves us in this direction.

For instance, after repeating the basic whole-body expansion meditation you learned in Chapter 2 many times, you will find that as soon as you turn your attention to your present breath experience, by habit your mind will bring you also into instant awareness of your heartbeat, your balance, your whole body at once. In just one breath, you come fully alive in the present moment.

I know that several of my old teachers would object to my encouraging you to turn a lengthy traditional meditation process into an instantaneous happening. But my personal experience has been that this new approach to meditation certainly has the blessing of the spiritual powers that be. In my own meditations, I am becoming more and more aware that we are being encouraged to approach meditation not as something to do just once or twice a day while in retreat, but also as something to do many times, quickly and yet deeply, while in the middle of whatever we are involved in at the moment.

The reality of contemporary life is that most of us simply don't have the luxury of a lot of free time on our hands to devote to kundalini awakening. We simply must find ways of quickly making kundalini contact in the midst of our hectic days—otherwise we make no contact at all. The Seven-Breath meditation is my understanding of how to merge ancient tradition with contemporary living.

Specifically, I am suggesting that you wake up your kundalini consciousness for at least a couple of minutes, optimally at least once an hour, by doing the Seven-Breath meditation I just taught you. This might seem a great challenge, but in practice it is not. You will feel such an instantaneous rush of positive, bright, transformed energy in your physical body and your mind when you do the Seven-Breath meditation that you will naturally begin to do it more and more often. We do gravitate toward pleasure, and kundalini meditation, when done right, does give us great pleasure.

As kundalini meditators, we find ourselves moving more and more into bliss in our everyday lives, simply because it feels good to move into the bliss. The psychological dynamics of habit formation are integral to the structure of this entire program. If we don't form the habit of regularly tapping into kundalini energy, we simply won't tap at all. So we must do our kundalini meditations so that they feel good, and thus reinforce our desire to do them again!

To complete the flow of this book, let me say what I said at the beginning—that it is awareness of our breathing experience that leads us toward bliss. If our breathing is consciously set free so it can move away from tensions and toward its natural bliss state, then the entire energetic system moves in this direction. It is always the initial act of turning our attention to our breathing that stimulates the movement toward at least momentary contact with kundalini bliss states.

Let me step aside and give you time and space to see again for yourself how your mind can effortlessly shift into higher levels of awareness.

Go ahead and gently do the whole-body expansion meditation, either in step-by-step fashion, or if you have memorized it, as an instantaneous process.

Focus first on the sensation of the air rushing in and out through your nose . . . the movement of your chest and belly as you breathe . . . your heartbeat or pulse . . . your sense of balance . . . your whole body here in the present moment . . . and expand your awareness to include all your chakras up and down your spine, at once!

## THE END IS WHERE WE START FROM

We are now reaching the end of your first linear exploration of the programs in this book. I hope you can already sense that I have written this book as a cyclic, spiraling experience, so that as you come to the end of your first reading, you naturally return to the beginning to discover the deeper dimensions that will open up to you as you encounter anew the first meditations you read about in this book.

Your next step in making kundalini meditation an integral part of your life will be to look back with more time and depth to each of the meditative processes. If I were teaching you these techniques in person, I would regularly point you back to the beginning steps, which as I mentioned earlier are also the ending steps.

I am going to now list formally five primary ways the various meditations you have learned in this book can be put together as a regular meditation session. You can choose which one or ones you want to memorize as a unit to use on an everyday basis. Feel free to modify these basic flows of meditative consciousness to suit your needs and preferences.

Evaluate the amount of time you have on hand for a meditative focusing of attention. Perhaps once or twice a day you have twenty to thirty minutes free for meditation. Perhaps three or four times a day you have five to ten minutes free to enjoy kundalini energy upsurges. Perhaps even ten times a day you have a couple of minutes free for kundalini charging and balancing. Take advantage of every free moment!

## Meditation One: The Seven-Breath Meditation
## (1 to 5 minutes)

I have described this meditation earlier in this chapter. It is one of the most easily accessible kundalini meditations for our modern age. I admit I have invented it on my own. My father was an inventor, and I am just a spiritual chip off the old block in this regard. I couldn't find any traditional meditation technique to fill this obvious void in our contemporary lives, so I have developed this one. My students and I have experimented with it for over twelve years, and find it extremely powerful and helpful. You can carry on with the new tradition.

I encourage you to do this meditation at least five times a day and, if possible, every half hour. Make it one of your most dearly treasured personal habits. A certain amount of discipline will be needed at first, but discipline can be a deeply satisfying experience. . . . Open up your daily schedule to short interludes where the kundalini spirit gets a specific chance to act through you—and let the habit take hold!

### *Meditation Two:* Pranayama *Breathing Session* *(5 to 30 minutes)*

It's important to do this meditation at least two or three times a week, for a full kundalini program.

(1) First, do the Energy-Pump meditation described on pages 98–99, which guides you into balancing your inhales and exhales.

(2) Then do the Kundalini-Rising breath meditation described on pages 120–121, to charge your kundalini system.

(3) Then do the Breath of Fire to further charge you, as described on page 141.

(4) Next do the *Pranayama* Alternate-Nostril Breathing, which balances the inflows of energy from above and below (pages 154–155).

(5) Finally, do the *Pranayama* Alternate-Nostril Breathing (pages 154–155) and the *Kumbhaka* breath meditations (pages 182–185), where you count inhales, hold breaths, and exhales to either balance, stimulate, or calm your energetic system. Meditate quietly in between each breath meditation and experience your chakras!

## *Meditation Three: Chanting Session (5 to 30 minutes)*

A number of chants are offered in this program, each of which can be done as a five-minute to half-hour meditation in itself, or in any combination.

At times it is a great pleasure to go through the seven-chakra meditation with a primary focusing on chanting. Put aside the other chakra meditations and enjoy a full chanting session, out loud, to awaken this dimension of your consciousness fully.

There are other times when you will find it deeply rewarding just to chant *OM* for a meditation session, be it two minutes or sixty.

Likewise, there will be times when you realize one of your chakras is low on energy, and you want to spend a few minutes or more chanting just that particular mantra for that chakra, to wake up energy in that realm of your life.

And certainly remember that the Humming Mantra should become a part of your everyday routines, bringing basic vibratory consciousness into everything you do.

## *Meditation Four: Mandala Session (10 to 30 minutes)*

Sometimes you will want to simply tune in to your breathing, your spine, your whole body at once, then quietly spend time meditating upon each of the seven mandalas in the book.

Focusing especially on the visual experience in meditation is both constructive in and of itself and also excellent training for effortlessly visualizing the mandalas in later meditations.

You can also focus just on one chakra or on a matched pair for a meditation session, employing the mandalas and mantras as a deep awakening of either masculine or feminine energies, depending on your present needs and desires.

*Meditation Five: Primary Daily Session*
*(20 to 60 minutes)*

Here we come to the full kundalini meditation, where you take plenty of time with each chakra, putting to use all four vehicles before moving on to the next chakra. To do this meditation at least once a day is optimal, preferably early in the morning, but at any other time if this is not possible.

The major thrust of this book has been to present this full meditation program. It can easily be extended into an hour meditation by going deeper into the four-vehicle meditations on each chakra and remaining longer in full-chakra consciousness at the end.

As with the other meditation programs I just outlined, you will of course need to go back into the text to memorize the procedures if you haven't already mastered them. For the full chakra meditation, Part II presents, chapter by chapter, the specific meditations. I hope you take time to master the entire seven-chakra process, since this is the heart of the entire kundalini program we've been learning.

## THE FULL SEVEN-CHAKRA KUNDALINI SESSION

As preparation, sit quietly, focus on your free breathing, and do the whole-body expansion meditation taught on page 50, to bring your attention fully into the present moment. Then move effortlessly through the flow of meditations listed below and on the following pages, referring to the text where necessary to refresh your memory.

**Chakra One**
>   Element: Earth
>   Focusing: Sphincter contraction (page 95)
>   Breathing: Energy-Pump (pages 98–99)
>   Mantra: *LAM* or *LANG* (pages 100–101)
>   Mandala: Four-petal (page 105)

**Chakra Two**
    Element: Water
    Focusing: Genital awakening (pages 124–125)
    Breathing: Kundalini-Rising (pages 120–121)
    Mantra: *VAM* or *VANG* (page 123)
    Mandala: Six-petal (page 126)

**Chakra Three**
    Element: Fire
    Focusing: Belly power (page 143)
    Breathing: Breath of Fire (page 141)
    Mantra: *RAM* or *RANG* (page 144)
    Mandala: Ten-petal (page 145)

**Chakra Four**
    Element: *Prana*/Air
    Focusing: The Cross (page 149)
    Breathing: *Pranayama* Alternate-Nostril
    (pages 154–155)
    Mantra: *YAM* or *YANG* (page 156)
    Mandala: Twelve-petal (page 160)

**Chakra Five**
    Element: Sound/Vibration
    Focusing: Humming (page 169)
    Breathing: Purification (page 168)
    Mantra: *HAM* or *HANG* (page 171)
    Mandala: Sixteen-petal (page 173)

**Chakra Six**
    Element: Light
    Focusing: The Third Eye (page 178)
    Breathing: *Kumbhaka* (pages 182–185)
    Mantra: *OM* or *AOUM* (page 185)
    Mandala: The *Ida-Pingala* (page 188)

## Chakra Seven

Element: Spirit
Focusing: Crown opening (page 193)
Breathing: Bliss (page 192)
Mantra: Silent *OM* (page 193)
Mandala: Crown-emanations (page 194)

Once you have practiced this routine, it will begin to come quite effortlessly to you, as you shift from one to the next meditation—they are in fact one great whole, each flowing into the next completely naturally. With each chakra, you simply focus on the location of the chakra, using the focusing meditation; then do the breathing meditation for that chakra; then the basic chant; then look at the mandala for the chakra or visualize it in your mind.

Go at whatever pace comes naturally to you with each chakra. When you have moved your kundalini energy up through all the chakras, simply breathe consciously for a while and experience whatever energy flows are happening in your system as a result of your meditation.

Also, open yourself to whatever new spirit encounter comes to you. You are now in the "receiving" mode of spiritual consciousness, where you commune with the deeper dimensions of the universe, and come face to face with your own indwelling divine presence. Enjoy!

And remember, when you end your meditation session, take this powerful, blissful, wise, loving, transformational spirit and share it freely with everyone you meet in your daily life. This is the true kundalini path that will transform the world—today!

# Final Words

*We've covered a great* deal of potent material in this book. Hopefully a time will come when you have digested everything I have taught and are ready to allow your own spiritual wisdom to begin to play "jazz variations" on the classical themes I have presented. This is perfectly fine and to be expected as you begin to allow the general formats of kundalini meditation to adapt to your own inner Master's suggestions—as the formats evolve in directions that match your personality and spiritual needs in the present moment.

The choice is always here—to direct our attention consciously for spiritual advancement or to let our attention fall victim to habitual patterns of inattentiveness. Use your primary spiritual tool of attention in such a way as to put the basic tools of kundalini meditation offered in this book to excellent and enjoyable use!

Keep in mind that you are free to awaken your awareness of your seven chakras—and lead yourself into the light and power of your kundalini energy—in any of the following situations: driving the kids to school, sitting in a waiting room, listening to a friend talking to you, reading a book such as this, watching the sun set, watching TV, walking down a busy city street, sitting at your computer or work desk, drinking a glass of wine at a restaurant, making love with your sexual partner, walking the dog, taking off in a jet airliner, jogging through the park, sitting on the proverbial pot, sitting in church, listening to the wind sighing in the trees, tying your shoes, taking a shower, falling asleep, falling from grace, mourning the loss of a loved one, meditating, breathing your very next breath . . .

Know that when you go into meditation, you are opening yourself to direct contact with your own inner Master, and all the spiritual Masters of all time—and also all other meditators on the earth. To consciously expand your consciousness to join in the great spiritual community of the present moment—this is the ultimate thrust of kundalini meditation.

In all our meditations, may we all meet regularly in seven-chakra consciousness, and join our souls and energies together so that we experience our shared planetary presence and shift from uncon-scious knowing of our oneness to a conscious, joyful sharing of our entrained vibrations, kundalini harmonies, and spiritual together-ness. Blessings, abundance and illumination—and a very good time along the way!

## FORMING YOUR OWN
## KUNDALINI-SUPPORT GROUP

Meditation is often considered a very personal, solitary experi-ence, and this is in many ways very true. However, I've found with my students and clients over the years that it can be extremely helpful to gather together in a compassionate support group, perhaps once a week, or even once a month, to share with a small circle of friends your experiences in exploring kundalini-awakening techniques.

It is also quite powerful to get together to meditate, to do the breath meditations and to chant together the mantras to the chakras, to move into a communal experience of each of the chakras and then of all the chakras at once, united through the silent *OM* that brings us into the universal realms of collective spiritual consciousness.

I recommend that you consider going into action, putting up notices around your community and perhaps in the paper as well, announcing a group spot where you invite people of like mind to gather to do kundalini meditations. You can use this book as the beginning focal point for the group if you want, and then allow your group to evolve in whatever directions suit your present meditation group needs.

## KUNDALINI RETREATS

Occasionally there are special kundalini retreats you might want to attend. If you have interest in an intensive meditation experience, you can write to:

Retreats with John Selby
P.O. Box 861
Kilauea, HI 96754

We have also prepared a special meditation-music tape, "Zen Tunes," which is available for twelve dollars at the above address. Letters describing your meditation experiences are also welcome.

## TRANSFORMATIONAL ART

All inquiries regarding Transformational Art and the visual tools of kundalini can be obtained by contacting:

Zachary Zelig Studios
1821 Wilshire Blvd., Suite 400
Santa Monica, CA 90403
(213) 828–1331

# Bibliography

Arguelles, Jose. *Mandala*. Shambala, 1972

Bartholomew. *I Come As a Brother*. High Mesa Press, Santa Fe, NM, 1986

Bentov, Itzhak. *Stalking the Wild Pendulum*. Fontana, 1977

*The Bhagavad-Gita*. Bantam, 1986

Blackney, Raymond. *Meister Eckhart*

Bohm, David. *Wholeness and the Implicate Order*

Capra, Fritjof. *The Tao of Physics*. Bantam, 1977

Castaneda, Carlos. *The Eagle's Gift*. Simon and Schuster, 1980

Castaneda, Carlos. *Tales of Power*. Simon and Schuster, 1975

Castaneda, Carlos. *The Teachings of Don Juan*. 1970

Chia, Mantak. *Taoist Secrets of Love*. Aurora Press, 1984

Colton, Anne Ree. *Kundalini West*. Ark Publ., 1978

Douglas, Nik and Slinger, Penny. *Sexual Secrets*. Destiny, 1979

Dubos, Rene. *Man, Medicine and Environment*. Praeger, 1968

Einstein, Albert. *The Evolution of Physics*. Simon and Schuster, 1961

Eliot, C. *Japanese Buddhism*. Barnes and Noble, 1969

Eliot, T. S. *Collected Poems 1909–1962*. Harcourt, 1963

Golas, Thaddeus. *The Lazy Man's Guide to Enlightenment.*
   Bantam 1972

Govinda, L. A. *Foundations of Tibetan Mysticism.* S. Weiser,
   1974

Graham, Dom Aelred. *Zen Catholicism*

Gulik, R. H. *Sexual Life in Ancient China.* E. J. Brill, 1974

Gurdjieff, G. *All and Everything.* E. P. Dutton, 1950

Heisenberg, W. *Physics and Beyond.* Harper, 1971

Hume, R. E. *The Thirteen Principal Upanishads.* Oxford
   University Press, 1934

Iyengar, B. K. *Light on Yoga.* Schoken Books, 1975

James, W. *Varieties of Religious Experience.* Longmans, 1935

Judith, Anodea. *Wheels of Life.* Llewellyn Publ., 1990

Jung, Carl. *Modern Man in Search of a Soul.* Harcourt, 1955

Koestler, Arthur. *The Act of Creation.* Random House, 1978

Kramer, Joel. *The Passionate Mind.* Celestial Arts, 1973

Krishna, Gopi. *Kundalini.* Shambala, 1985

Krishna, Gopi. *Kundalini for the New Age.* Bantam, 1988

Krishnamurti, J. *Freedom from the Known.* Harper, 1969

Lao-tzu. *Tao Te Ching.* Vintage Books, 1972

Lapleau, Roshiu Philip. *Zen.* Anchor, 1979

Lowen, Alexander. *Love and Orgasm.* Macmillan, 1965

May, Rollo. *Love and Will.* Norton, 1969

Muktananda, Swami. *Mystery of the Mind.* SYDA Foundation,
   1981

Muller, F. M. *Buddhist Mahayana Sutras.* Oxford University
   Press, 1955

Ouspensky, P. D. *In Search of the Miraculous*

Pagels, Elaine. *The Gnostic Gospels.* Random House, 1979

Payne, Roger. "Whales." *The New Yorker,* February 26, 1990

Pearce, Joseph Chilton. *Bond of Power.* E. P. Dutton, 1981

Pearce, Joseph Chilton. *Magical Child.* E. P. Dutton, 1977

Pearce, Joseph Chilton. *Magical Child Matures.* Bantam, 1986

Prem, Krishna. *The Yoga of the Kathopanishad.* Watkins, 1955

Rajneesh, B. S. *The Mustard Seed*. Harper, 1975

Reich, Wilhelm. *The Function of the Orgasm*. P. Wolf, 1971

Sannella, Lee. *Kundalini-Psychosis or Transcendence*. Dakin, 1976

Schweitzer, Albert. *Out of My Life and Thought*. Holt, 1949

Selby, John. *Conscious Healing*. Bantam, 1991

Selby, John. *Peak Sexual Experience*. Warner Books, 1992

Selby, John. *The Visual Handbook*. Element Books, London, 1987

Shaw, Idres. *The Way of the Sufi*. E. P. Dutton, 1968

Singh, J. *The Siva Sutras*. Motilal Publ., Delhi, 1979

Smith, Morton. *The Secret Gospel*

Suzuki, D. T. *Indian Mahayana Buddhism*. Harper, 1968

*The Teaching of Buddha*. Kosaido Publ., Tokyo, 1980

Thomas, Lewis. *The Lives of a Cell*. Bantam, 1974

Tulku, Tarthang. *Time, Space, and Knowledge*. Darma Publ., 1977

Vivekananda, S. *Jnana Yoga*. Ramakrishna Center Press, 1972

Watts, Alan. *Nature, Man and Woman*. Thames Hudson, 1958

Watts, Alan. *This Is It*. Penguin Books, 1977

Watts, Alan. *The Way of Zen*. Vintage Books, 1957

West, Anthony. *The High Wisdom of Egypt*

Woodroffe, John. *The Serpent Power*. 9th ed. Ganesh Press, 1973

Wyman, Alan. *The Buddhist Tantras*. Routledge, London, 1973

Yogananda, P. *Autobiography of a Yogi*. Self-Realization, 1946

Zimmer, H. *Myths in Indian Civilization*. Pantheon, 1963

Zukav, Gary. *The Dancing Wu Li Masters*. Bantam, 1980